Copyright © 2022 Emily Ridout

All rights reserved. No part of this book may be reproduced or transmitted in any form or by any means electronic or mechanical including photocopying, recording, or by any information storage and retrieval system without permission in writing from the publisher or author.

Aurora Books, an imprint of Eco-Justice Press, L.L.C.

Aurora Books
P.O. Box 5409 Eugene, OR 97405
www.ecojusticepress.com

AstroYoga for an Aquarian Age
Cover illustration Alejandro Sarmiento with Eco-Justice Press

Library of Congress Control Number: 2023930969
ISBN 978-1-945432-53-8

AstroYoga for an Aquarian Age

Emily Ridout

Table of Contents

Chapter 1: What is AstroYoga? 9

Chapter 2: The Luminaries and Yoga 23

Chapter 3: An Energetic Understanding of the Zodiac 33

Chapter 4: Who are the Planets? 45

Chapter 5: The Zodiac, Planets, and the Physical Body 69

Chapter 6: The Zodiac, Planets, and the Subtle Body 101

Chapter 7: Houses, Aspects, and Reading the Natal Chart 117

Chapter 8: Planning Your AstroYoga Practice 135

Introduction

This book has sprouted and lived within me for the past 13 years, as I researched, studied, and integrated these practices into my life.

I am of the belief that the many paths we walk all eventually lead to the same place. Of the paths available, some are more direct than others, and some are more suitable to particular personalities than others.

My research, personal and professional practice, and exploration in this field constitute a historical and modern reckoning of the two paths I've walked, one from the Western schools and one from the Eastern schools. In every detail, I've committed to using truths from these two traditions, albeit occasionally esoteric ones that might not be apparent to the casual observer.

Above all else, what I'm discussing in this book is the character of time itself and its correspondence to the many layers of your being. How your physical and energetic form is positioned in time and space has everything to do with your life, and AstroYoga will show you how to dance with time, consciousness, and energy in a way that promotes your ever-unfolding wellbeing and success in your endeavors.

The dedicated student of astrology and yoga will eventually arrive at a place where these systems no longer feel like the hard-won knowledge of study and the concentration of the mind, but instead will feel like an effortless focus applied to the embodied dance of life. Additionally, the apparent differences between seemingly separate approaches (sidereal to tropical; intellectual to embodied; Eastern to Western) will eventually disappear as personal perceptions and pedantic preferences give way to the clear, single reality of Truth.

This book is meant to be read straight through, which differentiates it from many astrology books that encourage use as reference materials. Although, for ease of use, reference tables are given throughout.

I am in gratitude to so many beings who offered me encouragement, inspiration, teachings, practices, and light in my personal journey along this path. To my teachers, family, and friends, thank you. You are the reason I've written these words.

Acknowledgments

When I think about life during the process of writing this book, I feel immense gratitude. This writing, editing, and publishing process has made palpable the truth that each of us is inextricably tied to a network of beings who both help to shape us and also make life worthwhile.

The first person I have to thank is my mom, Susan Ridout, without whom none of this would be written. Not only did she give me life, but she also listened to me speak on this topic for years and then proceeded to edit the manuscript with the precision and grace she brings to everything.

I also have Kurt Alford, Lauren Hack, Lindsay Hack, and my dad, Kyle Ridout, to thank for reading manuscripts and offering me constructive feedback. Their perspectives and holistic thoughts altered this book for the better, and I am grateful for the many hours spent pouring over these words and encouraging me to put this work out into the world.

I'm grateful to Ashley Steinmetz, my long-time business advisor, whose focus is perpetually on the quality and integrity of the soul, and who has blessed my life and my yoga teaching in so many ways.

As well, this book is possible through the diligence of my publisher, David Diethelm, and through the talents of Alejandro Sarmiento, who so perfectly did the cover art.

For the images inside the book, there are several people to thank. I wouldn't have photos to use if it weren't for Benjamin Wilkinson, who both provided the studio space and took many of the photos in this book. For the author photo, I have Krista Rossow to thank for her photography skills and also her ability to find a sunny day in the Eugene winter. As well, many of the graphics in this book are made possible through Artulina, Jessica Aceret, Blixa 6 Studios, and Nomad Visuals Co. via Canva.com.

And of course, I'm grateful to my teachers on my path and to their teachers. To my friends, colleagues, clients, and community members, I am grateful to you. This line of work has given me the incredible benefit of being in contact with so many great souls who inspire and connect me to purpose beyond myself.

Chapter 1: What is AstroYoga?

Key Points in this Chapter
- AstroYoga is the combination of yoga and astrology.
- Astrology is the primary basis we have for time.
- Astrology is number in time and space, which follows a harmonic, fractal understanding of the universe.
- Yoga includes practices familiar to many modern practitioners, but also includes an understanding of the physical, mental, and mystical shifts that take place as a result of practice.
- AstroYoga connects the cosmic principles in astrology to their physiological and spiritual components in the human form.
- There are two predominant approaches to time in AstroYoga: sidereal time related to stars and tropical time related to angles among planets. Both forms of time are relevant. I encourage beginners to begin with tropical time.

Astrology + Yoga = AstroYoga

Although I have been engaged in this field for 13 years, I have a confession to make: when I first learned of the astrology-yoga connection during my yoga studies in Hyderabad, India, I thought it sounded absurd. In fact, I found it so unbelievable that I set out to disprove astrology's validity.

You can probably already guess that like so many who doubt the wisdom present in yoga, I found that I was the mistaken one, not the teachers and texts that hold this knowledge. As I set to my task, it was only a matter of months until I proved to myself that not only was this field valid, but that it was shocking in its accuracy and usefulness. Over the next eight years, I set out to learn all I could about it, and eventually opened a professional practice in this field in 2016.

The need for this book emerges largely from the fact that, while most of us know the words astrology and yoga, these words point to a subject matter so vast and deep that no single human in a lifetime could exhaust the full knowledge of what their symbolism and practices entail. The picture each of us has in our heads of AstroYoga at first—or second, or one-hundredth—glance is necessarily incomplete. Yet, progress can be made on this topic, if you have the interest.

Both systems are interrelated in a way that reveals important truths about the body, the Self, and the human place in the grand scheme of things. When understood individually, one system reveals the other. When studied in tandem, great strides can be made along the path of self-realization.

Studying AstroYoga can involve a great deal of 'unlearning' as you reframe cultural contexts and apply esoteric organizational principles to ordinary experiences in life. As well, studying AstroYoga can encourage you to take control of your own life experience by aligning with and embodying the fullness of reality.

So, astrology plus yoga is AstroYoga, but before we move beyond this deceptively simple statement, take a moment to consider what both astrology and yoga truly are.

Moving from Exoteric Knowledge to Esoteric Understanding

In this book, many references are made to philosophies, religions, and cultures in antiquity and the modern era. Many of these may be familiar to you. What is broadly known about these topics is considered to be an exoteric level of understanding. Exoteric understanding equates to commonplace knowledge. Exoteric knowledge alone may make a philosophy, religion, or custom seem confusing or even absurd to the outside observer, since the deeper meanings remain hidden in symbols. However, what this book aims to cover is the esoteric. Esoteric understanding differs from the exoteric in that esoteric concepts are hidden. Esoteric, or hidden, knowledge is concealed either because its profundity may be unacceptable to the larger culture, or because its depth is beyond what may be described with words. So when words are insufficient, the esoteric is described with symbols.

Symbolic systems in culture, philosophy, and religion point to the truths hidden in plain sight that are for each of us to uncover somewhere along the human journey. As we move into the Aquarian Age, several layers of the esoteric are becoming available to the general public. This book is meant to be a guide for those beginning to uncover the esoteric symbolism and knowledge in AstroYoga.

Astrology

Put simply, astrology is the cultural component of astronomy.

This definition is purposefully broad because at its core, astrology is so much more than the horoscopes and charts that many associate with it. Like many deep subjects, knowledge about astrology and yoga can be divided into the esoteric (hidden practices and meanings) and the exoteric (mundane practices and meanings).

Exoteric astrology originally developed for purely practical reasons. Our earliest ancestors used astrology to do things such as know when to hunt, fish, plant, and harvest food. Once basic needs were met with astrology, it likely informed groups on when to time their spiritual and religious celebrations. Still today, most major religions operate within a hybrid solar/lunar calendar. It was later on that astrology started being applied to interpersonal issues as groups vied for political power and competed for other resources. Medical astrology gained widespread use that persisted through the Age of Reason, and of course the natal horoscope was used to examine the lives of individuals, events, and groups.

While exoteric astrology had widespread historical use, esoteric astrology is more relevant to the study of AstroYoga. Esoteric schools dating back to times before record used astrology as a means to accomplish what is often called the Great Work, which is essentially perfecting the individual consciousness by uniting it with higher levels of awareness. It's these esoteric schools that tie astrology and yoga together.

One key fact about astrology that many overlook is that astrology is the primary basis we have for time. Let this concept fully develop in your mind, and take the time to consider what it means. Because astrology represents any human cultural interaction with the cosmos, without astrology we have no concept of day and night, because the relationship of the Sun to Earth dictates these periods. Without the Moon, the concept of month (moon-th) does not exist. And of course, hours (named for Horus the Egyptian solar deity), minutes, and seconds are all dependent on these periods. Our concept of a week comes from days named for the seven visible planets, inclusive of the two luminaries, the Sun and Moon.

The concept of time will come up again and again as you study astrology, because one of the biggest human interactions with astrology is simply this: our experience with time, clocks, and calendars.

You can think of astrology as a particularly special clock that tells you not just what time, month, year, or age it is, but also something about the character of that particular time.

This is useful in two ways.

First, it assists you in the same way that knowing a person offers you some degree of expectation regarding your experience. If you meet a stranger, you may feel a bit on edge, wondering if you are to meet a friend or foe. If you know you're set to meet your old friend, family member, or colleague, you'll prepare accordingly. Likewise, when you know the sort of time you're in, you can prepare yourself to rise to meet the moment.

Second, knowing a time's character allows you to see time for what it is: a dimension which binds humanity, but also a dimension which can be explored to see into the true nature of reality. By understanding the nature of the very thing that binds us, we may eventually set ourselves free. This concept will be clearer the more thoroughly you explore the esoteric relationship of planets to the zodiac and the body. As you study AstroYoga, carefully consider the nature of time and your place within it.

How Does Astrology Work?

Inevitably, the question of how astrology works arises in the careful consideration of time itself. While it's not the scope of this book to go deeply into this topic, it's essential to understand a few points regarding this quandary.

Put simply, astrology is an application of number when applied to four dimensions: length, height, depth, and time. Astrology works similarly to harmonics, which is also the application of number in four dimensions. Though we can notice four dimensions acutely, more are implied. As you deepen your studies, additional dimensions may be explored in their relationship to AstroYoga to magnify your understanding of the influence of number beyond the material, temporal plane.

When I was in my mid-20s, I taught voice and music theory at a music conservatory, and I always loved this example, which demonstrates how harmonic resonance operates in perception, time, and space.

The story goes that a vocalist heard the most beautiful and resonant high soprano coming from somewhere in a building he was walking through. He decided he must know which singer was making such a beautiful high note. As he walked, the tone grew deeper, and he eventually discovered, not a soprano, but a baritone.

When a note sounds in perfect resonance, the originating note has a series of overtones which mathematically emerge in predictable intervals. Likewise, the resonances present in the cosmos have corresponding predictable patterns here on Earth. This resonant patterning of astrology works on many levels:

- The macro level (nations, peoples, world events)
- The interpersonal level (happenings in our lives and the lives of those around us)
- The personal level (our physical and energetic bodies and minds)
- The micro level (the cellular makeup of our forms and minutia, of which we are often unaware)

The roots of astrologic influences exist at a fundamental level of reality, only one level of which is the cosmos we track in astrology. As the universe unfolds, multiple levels of reality operate harmonically with one another. That is to say that mathematically, what is happening in the cosmos is resolutely also occurring within the cells of your body, interpersonally among human beings, and within your own mind.

Astrology operates on a vibratory spectrum which may be understood as the harmonics of sound or as the spectrum and refraction of light. There is a vibratory level at which sound, light, and time merge. With a finely attuned instrument, it may be possible to see sound and hear light. Careful exploration of this topic will give you clear insights into the mechanism by which astrology and the universe operate. When you understand the nature of harmonics, space, and time, you have an excellent window into the echo-chamber that is the manifest world interacting with the cosmos.

Yoga

Yoga has been defined, redefined, and personalized by many experts and yoga students throughout the years. People often define the word yoga based on the Sanskrit root yuj, which means to yoke, a word that implies tying the body and spirit to each other through the mechanism of right discipline.

This is, of course, a useful definition, and one that already aligns yoga to some esoteric schools of astrology. Such schools associate the zodiac sign Taurus with acts of esoteric spirituality, meditation, and the symbol of yoking the self-aware individual consciousness with the higher levels of universal consciousness. Yet to truly define yoga, we must also give deep credit to India and her many enlightened teachers.

Each person who practices yoga is indebted to a series of teachers who benevolently kept a safe harbor for these initiatory practices throughout millennia. Yoga is perhaps the system of esotericism most available and open to people in the world today, and as such, all modern yoga practitioners can bow deeply to the teachers and lineages that brought these practices to us.

Yoga is a word broadly applied to include physical postures (asana), breath patterns (pranayama), energetic seals (mudra), the uttering of specific vibratory syllables (mantra and japa), and the act of meditation. The important thing is growing conscious of the life within and around you. If you can do this fully, the act of yoga will be your act of living.

How Does Yoga Work?

People have spent entire lifetimes seeking a satisfactory answer to this question, and so by no means will these few paragraphs offer anything that could comprehensively describe the topic. However, it is my hope that through a brief framing of this topic, you'll have the basis necessary to understand yoga and the means by which it necessarily relates to astrology.

Yoga is a process where the personal human consciousness seeks to become aware of the modes of consciousness that allow for greater states of freedom, or svatantra in Sanskrit.

Through techniques distinct to various schools of yoga, the great yogis laid out systems of understanding that intellectually model the universe as vibratory in nature, moving from the subtlest forms of sound or light and into the grossest. At a high level, these techniques give the practitioner direct experience of subtle layers of conscious expression. Though these experiences are beyond the present grasp of most people today, humanity as a whole is preparing to step more fully into experiencing these layers of consciousness, which are available to all of us when we seek them.

Given these intellectual models inherited from the great yogi sages, practitioners of yoga seek to animate the physical and chemical structures in their bodies to move toward greater and greater states of conscious awareness.

This is a key concept in AstroYoga. The means by which yoga works is spiritual, yes, but there are literal, often measurable, physical and chemical shifts that take place in the body. Previously unused and underdeveloped parts of the brain become active, the chemical makeup of the blood shifts, and the person becomes more conscious.

From an outside perspective, this can make the fully developed yogi seem to possess super-human capabilities, though in many cases sages insist that such capabilities are in fact available to all who would walk the path of yoga.

AstroYoga

Astrology and yoga have evolved both independently and interdependently. You could fill several volumes of books just with the history of yoga and the history of astrology. Both disciplines date back at least four thousand years, yet the manner in which they are practiced has radically shifted over time. There are also certain principles that remain timelessly unchanged, if you know where and how to look.

To discuss the concept of AstroYoga means to discuss disciplines that span time and space. These disciplines primarily intersected along the Indo-European trade route, with deep bows to India for keeping the yogic tradition alive, and to Egypt and the Middle East for being hubs for astrology in the ancient world. Studying AstroYoga requires being open to the esoteric mystery traditions which house these disciplines.

On the surface, astrology, yoga, and AstroYoga may appear to be lighthearted disciplines that anyone may try before moving on to the next fad. However, if you take the time to deeply consider what AstroYoga offers, you're sure to discover a treasure trove of information and practices that can facilitate your healing, self-actualization, and the manifestation of your desires.

Throughout the sacred texts of the ancient world, we find references to ideas that imply that the creation and unfoldment of 'heaven' is possible on Earth. Sages and religious analysts alike have made reference to the concept of a time when humanity would live in harmony: heaven on Earth. Almost universally, when you trace these linguistic references back through time, you find the original meaning implies humanity is living in accordance with the heavens, or cosmic order. In other words, the foretold time of harmony, often thought to be the burgeoning Aquarian Age, is a direct reference to humanity living in true accordance with the timing of astrology.

What is AstroYoga except the practice of aligning the body with your personal astrology as well as the astrology of the present moment? The practice of AstroYoga aligns the physical energies of the body with the more subtle energies of the character of time.

When you truly grasp this concept, you'll never fail to see how essential AstroYoga will be in the age to come. AstroYoga teaches that by aligning yourself in harmony with the cosmos, you do your part to align the whole of humanity with the cosmos. After all, the piece of humanity you are personally responsible for is yourself.

This is an important point, and one that many could overlook as new-age jargon, but there is significant truth in it. Test it out for yourself. When you are joyful, aligned, healthy, and facing challenge with courage, the world does in fact become just a little better. This is most directly felt in your subjective experience and the experiences of those around you.

To step fully into the Aquarian Age, each individual must truly grasp what 'live and let live' means, simultaneously accepting personal responsibility while releasing the tempting habit of projection that plagues so many of us.

This process is for the courageous. If you start down this path, the surface levels of AstroYoga will quickly offer you ways to align with what you want, as well as provide some degree of physical wellbeing. But as you continue and deepen your practice, you will feel the draw to not only solve your most obvious problems in life, but to actually accept the true wonder of what you are—a unique and whole individual on multiple planes of reality. To live your truth and embody your most magnificent self, you will be faced with the challenge of healing that which has kept you from that truth. This is a process, and different individuals will experience this in various ways, from gentle to abrupt.

How Does AstroYoga Work?

AstroYoga works by the same mechanisms as astrology and yoga when they are practiced fully. If you progress far enough with either discipline on its own, you'll wind up in a deep study and contemplation of the other; this is because they've never truly been separate, only presented as such in certain arenas.

AstroYoga has the distinct niche of presenting both the theoretical knowledge needed to examine oneself and one's place in the world, as well as the practices that can support the positive unfolding of oneself though time.

Human beings are not stagnant, stable creatures. We emerge as babies, and grow into youths, adults, and elders that hardly resemble our past forms. Along the way, we learn lessons through experience, study, and observation, and the manifestation of who we naturally are grows along with us.

AstroYoga offers the useful practices and understandings necessary to support individuals as they align with themselves where they are in their journey, make progress toward their natural unfoldment, and connect with the broader spirit of the present moment of time.

The well-known hermetic principle of correspondence is at play here: as above so below, as below so above. A human being lives within the cosmos, and each individual is a microcosm, a tiny universe. Like the larger universe, an individual experiences shifts in physical and energetic pieces of the inner and outer world that correspond in time and character to the larger cosmos.

Essentially, a skilled AstroYoga practitioner can tell what is going on within an individual or in the world at large by careful observation of the cosmos. A skilled AstroYoga practitioner will also be able to note what is going on in the cosmos through careful observation of the world or their own internal state. The vibratory, harmonic, fractal nature of the universe is observable on many levels when the human instrument is finely tuned. AstroYoga approaches this truth from both ends, in order to attune the individual with practices and to apply right theory through the lens of thoughtful observation and study.

I hope you find some helpful mechanisms in these pages by which to consider your own conscious unfolding in harmony with the dimensions of time and space.

A Word on Time

Earlier in this chapter, I mentioned that astrology is the primary basis we have for time. This understanding opens the door for considering multiple systems of time, as well as their relationships with one another.

In astrology, time can be controversial between two schools of thought. The two prevailing approaches to time are tropical and sidereal.

Tropical time is primarily concerned with the angles among planets, especially the angular relationship between the Sun and Earth. Sidereal time is time as related to the stars. Its primary concern is the play of celestial objects, such as planets and luminaries, as related to the backdrop of the stars and constellations. This zodiacal backdrop shifts slowly over the ages, when compared to the seasons and calendar year.

Both tropical and sidereal time are correct and useful; they simply have different reference points. These different reference points have been the source of more than a little confusion when an individual first explores astrology.

In tropical time, the zodiac is determined by mathematical angles among planets. This places emphasis on the appearance of the Sun's movement from the Equator to the Tropic of Cancer, back to the Equator and to the Tropic of Capricorn. What this means is that every year at the vernal equinox the Sun sits at zero degrees of Aries, no matter where the constellation of Aries sits in the sky. In other words, the zodiac is more related to the seasons of the year and patterns of life than to the constellations.

In sidereal time, the zodiac is determined by the literal constellations on the zodiacal belt. This places emphasis on particular stars and constellations. What this means is that every year at the vernal equinox the Sun sits at a slightly different place in the zodiac, changing signs about every 2000 years. Relative to Earth, the zodiacal belt moves slowly over time. In sidereal time, the emphasis is on the predominating influence of the stars, regardless of the seasons and patterns of life on Earth.

Both systems have value, and the influx of stellar influence is viewable in each, simply through different perspectives. By studying both, you'll come to understand the precession of the equinoxes as the connection between sidereal and tropical time, which serves to complete our understanding of time as it relates to life on Earth.

That being said, with some exceptions, sidereal time has largely been favored in traditions from India, and tropical time has often been favored in the West. This is not always the case, but until one understands how to fluently read both, it's important to understand biases and limitations when reading from a singular system.

The character of time has many influences and is informed by the combination of tropical and sidereal time. If you only examine tropical time, then history appears as cyclical. While there is a cyclical aspect to life, it's more true that life is cycling as a spiral, constantly expanding and co-creating the future with past versions of itself. The combination of sidereal and tropical astrology offers a distinct perspective of not only a snapshot of time but also how we are evolving with and influencing time. This mutual co-evolution and co-influence of humanity and time is the premise upon which the burgeoning Aquarian Age is based.

The reconciliation of tropical and sidereal time is one area where my work is distinct. I choose to read astrology with an understanding of both tropical and sidereal time, since both are always at play. Tropical time is the most apparent to us locally since it aligns with the seasons and movements of the Sun, but this all plays out against a sidereal backdrop that slowly unfolds. The reconciliation of tropical and sidereal interpretation eventually leads to the understanding that the wheel of time is not so much of a circular wheel as it is a spiral, always spinning us into the unfurling characteristics of new ages in conscious unfolding.

For the purposes of this book, I'll mainly be discussing tropical time, as it tends to be the time system most people today are familiar with in the cultural context in which I live. As well, those who study nuance and various systems of chart calculation will recognize that certain approaches to tropical charts offer a more mathematically accurate landscape upon which to add sidereal time. This makes for easier reading and chart interpretation than beginning with the whole-house approach traditional to many forms of sidereal astrology, and then adding in tropical time later, although this approach is also legitimate.

I'm sure my decision to include tropical charts in my examples is not without controversy, as in some respects it diverges from the general use of sidereal time when applied to yoga. My intention is in no way to discredit the important influence of sidereal time as related to AstroYoga, but to share a complex perspective that is inclusive of both modes of time awareness.

Tropical and Sidereal Solar Transit Dates		
Zodiac Sign	Tropical	Sidereal
Aries	March 21-April 19	April 14-May 14
Taurus	April 20-May 20	May 15-June 15
Gemini	May 21-June 20	June 16-July 16
Cancer	June 21-July 22	July 17-August 16
Leo	July 23-August 22	August 17-September 16
Virgo	August 23-September 22	September 17-October 17
Libra	September 23-October 22	October 18-November 16
Scorpio	October 23-November 21	November 17-December 15
Sagittarius	November 22-December 21	December 16-January 14
Capricorn	December 22-January 19	January 15-February 12
Aquarius	January 20-February 18	February 13-March 14
Pisces	February 19-March 20	March 15-April 13
The sidereal dates change slightly over time. These dates are based on the Lahiri Ayanamsha of 24 degrees.		

How to Use AstroYoga

The casual reader can use AstroYoga in a number of ways.

The first, and most obvious, is to use principles of AstroYoga to practice in accordance with the timing of the cosmos and seasons. This includes things like paying attention to the current transits, adjusting flows for lunation cycles, and knowing how the changing seasons affect the practice of yoga. For example, when the moon is new or full the practitioner may choose to practice lunar varieties of yoga, such as chandra namaskar, the moon salute. Likewise, on solstices a practitioner may practice 108 surya namaskars, or sun salutes. If the yoga practitioner is aware of other transits among planets, these may also be incorporated.

The second way to use AstroYoga is to apply specific yoga practices to an individual chart. This can include acts of integration and self actualization through the process of 'waking up' or integrating a planetary energy that is either over- or under-expressed. This method can also include acts of balancing an individual's chart based on what is observed in the body, or directly addressing granthis (energetic knots) that are ready to be loosened to restore the flow of prana.

The third way to use AstroYoga is a combination of the two other ways, balancing an individual according to the natal chart as well as according to the present-moment transits that are affecting their chart. Though this method has the most layers, it's also the most comprehensive method.

Three Basic Ways To Practice AstroYoga

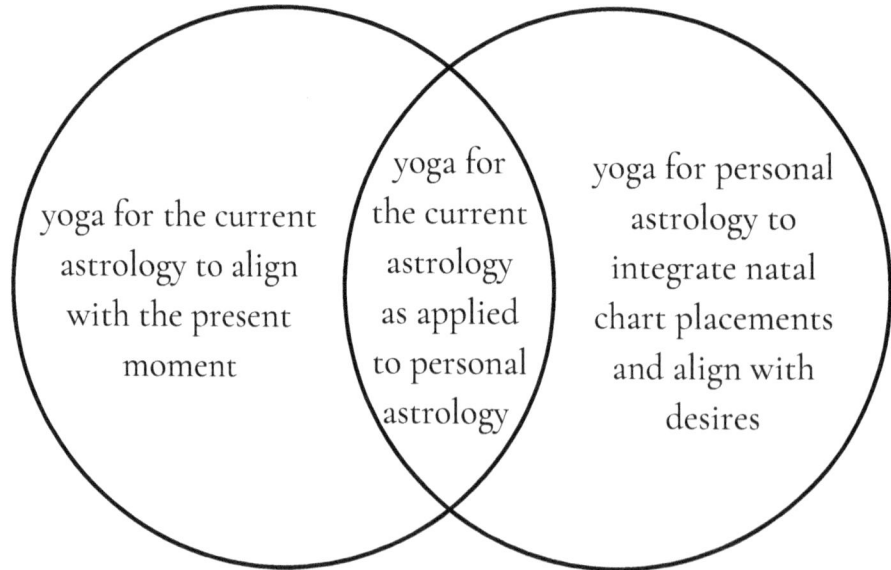

Ultimately, most yoga practitioners are on a householder path, meaning they are living in the world, maintaining work and relationships while they dive into their yoga practices. This path will include desire at many points; most people who come to the practice of AstroYoga have something they want. They may want harmony, happiness, and growth in their personal life, relationships, finances, careers, spiritual path, family relationships, creative life, community endeavors, or other arenas.

Each person's natal chart shows the conditions for harmony and happiness that must be present for them to find satisfaction in particular areas of life. AstroYoga is a practice that, when rightly applied, can call the necessary energies to the individual in a way that creates the systematic unfolding of success which is specific to that individual's patterning.

To me, this is something special. The first step is knowing what you want. AstroYoga offers the gift of practicing in such a manner that you're ready to receive exactly what it is you've envisioned for yourself. Practice in alignment with your deep desire, and watch how good things unfold in your life.

Chapter 2: The Luminaries and Yoga

Key Points in this Chapter
- The luminaries are the Sun and Moon.
- The solar principle represents superconscious awareness, while the lunar principle represents subconscious power.
- The luminaries relate to the nadis or energy channels of the subtle body.
- Working with the luminaries in your AstroYoga practice can create positive shifts in layers of your consciousness and in your life experience.

What are Luminaries?

In astrology, the Sun and Moon are called luminaries. They light up the chart and our lives so we can see clearly. The root lumin is Latin for light, and Aries is the sign which rules inner and outer vision. Thus the luminaries are lights that create the conditions for both clarifying your vision and enacting your vision for your life.

In the study of AstroYoga, every astrological influence is operational on multiple levels of reality, which both include and transcend the physical and energetic levels of our experience. The Sun and Moon are of the utmost importance in this regard. Their operation is at play on multiple levels of reality. Of course, there are the Sun and Moon that we observe in the sky. There are also solar and lunar aspects of human personality, the physical body, and the energetic auric light that a person gives off.

To merely think you know what the Sun and Moon are is not enough. The secrets contained within these two luminaries are vast, and deep study and practice will continually shine more light on the matter.

The Sun and Moon as Cosmic Lovers

Though there are many stories of love in the zodiac, the Sun and Moon are the first and most essential pair of cosmic lovers.

The Sun and Moon are complementary principles of consciousness and light that operate on a scale of polarity. One consequence of the dance of the luminaries is that these forms of light consciousness are operational throughout reality. The interaction of the solar and lunar principles are at play in specific human aims including such varied tasks as igniting a lightbulb, moving the human body, or doing the work of studying AstroYoga. Essentially the polarity between the luminaries creates the energetic motion that is life on every level, and there is no aspect of human life in which these two luminaries are not at play.

These luminaries operate as an energetic continuum of light, but operate in different polarities of that light. The Sun and Moon are opposite poles in terms of energy (the Sun operates as electricity, the Moon as magnetism); sequentiality (the Sun initiates energy, the Moon reflects it); functionality (the Sun radiates energy and warmth in an observable way, the Moon draws connections in ways that can't always be seen or measured); and gender (the Sun operates in a masculine polarity, the Moon in a feminine polarity).

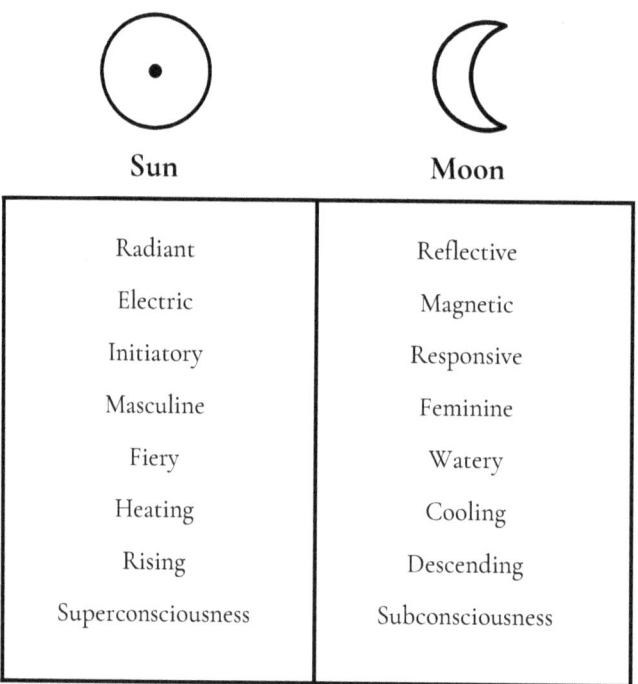

Sun	Moon
Radiant	Reflective
Electric	Magnetic
Initiatory	Responsive
Masculine	Feminine
Fiery	Watery
Heating	Cooling
Rising	Descending
Superconsciousness	Subconsciousness

The Sun and Moon operate as gendered polarities, but the idea of gender in astrology has some degree of nuance compared to thinking about personal gender. There is a cultural phenomenon where personal gender expression is being examined and reexamined, defined and redefined. Though the word gender is used in both astrology and in personal gender expression, what we are talking about has little to do with an individual's gender expression or identity.

To understand these principles is not to understand men and women, but rather to understand the principles of consciousness at play within each person and in the world outside the individual.

The dance of the cosmic lovers is taking place outside you and inside you, and the masculine and feminine principles become valuable tools to work with in AstroYoga. It is useful to understand what the terms masculine and feminine mean in astrology. Essentially, the concepts of masculine and feminine reference specific forms of consciousness, the modes of which are present in every human being. These forms of consciousness are either masculine (heating, radiating, directing, and operating in a realm of self-conscious observation) or feminine (cooling, condensing, nurturing, and operating in a realm of subconscious movement and power).

So, the Sun and Moon are the masculine and feminine principles of light, respectively. Regardless of personal gender expression, the solar and lunar principles are ideally integrated within the chart of every individual; this will not inherently make you more 'masculine' or 'feminine,' but you might find it removes layers of cultural masking and aligns you with your most natural inner state.

 The Solar Principle

The solar principle, when considered as the Sun we see in the sky, represents the light of consciousness itself: the enlightening, life-enhancing, essential principle that offers the seed of infinite potential.

In a person's natal chart the solar principle represents the degree and manner in which the individual becomes aware of and expresses their individual allotment of solar energy, which is derived from the Sun. This is an important point. The Sun that you see in the sky is responsible for the construction and perpetuation of life on Earth. The Sun is the initial spark that creates this life, making possible photosynthesis that creates air and nutrition, both of which are the building blocks of the physical human body.

The solar principle, when considered in the individual chart, represents how and what an individual does with their measure of solar energy that is embodied within them and being expressed through them.

When the solar principle shows up within a person, the light of conscious awareness will be offered according to that person's individual will, desires, and level of consciousness. Though the same solar energy animates all beings, the outlets for solar energy can be wisely applied, squandered, or directed/misdirected. The solar energy as the radiant force can be wisely applied in such a way that promotes living life in a state of enlightenment. This realized solar state is conducive to abundance, awareness, and overall wellbeing. When squandered or misdirected, the radiant solar force lives in a state of suffering, forgetting its originating light. This misdirected or squandered state either gives light to negative life experiences or dampens the internal light.

To properly integrate the solar principle in the body requires a connection to and understanding of the character of your own consciousness. Understanding the character of your own consciousness is a primary theme in yoga. This includes a nuanced view of the persona you have constructed of yourself. When examining your persona, it's important to understand that our ideas about ourselves are generally incomplete. This incomplete self-knowledge stems from selective remembering, thought patterns, and habitual states of emotion that create a narrative about who we think we are. It is challenging to accurately include the sum total of all thoughts, feelings, attitudes, and actions that make up a human persona, but the more you can do this, the closer you'll be to realizing your solar principle.

The solar principle is important in the chart because this is the part of you that inherently knows your own enlightenment. You may have heard in yoga that all beings are already enlightened, most have just forgotten their true identity. As we grow more specific, we grow more useful in various circumstances, but we also forget the full splendor of our infinite nature. Even though the infinite light still permeates our beings, we forget this essential piece of our nature. To illustrate this point, consider that raw clay has infinite possibilities, but the coffee mug is what you reach for when you need a vessel from which to drink. Limitation begets usefulness, but also temporarily blinds us to the scope of the infinite.

This truth is nothing to mourn over, but something to be aware of as you work with this piece of your chart that represents enlightenment. As you continue in your AstroYoga work, you'll find there are mental and physiological shifts that take place when the solar principle is properly integrated.

On one level, the Sun represents the light of superconscious awareness, although in most individuals in the current age this is operational only in part. When the solar principle is partially operational, the individual glimpses something of their own inner light, and creates a persona construct that elaborates the partial reality they have understood. Sometimes this elaborated reality is referred to as ego, however both the words ego and self-consciousness have been used in various contexts that obfuscate their original meanings.

For the purposes of AstroYoga, the solar principle is twofold. On the lower level, it represents the constructed sense of self that is referred to as ego. This is initially an idea that a person has about who and what they are, and later it may become an embodied state where the light of superconscious awareness is made manifest. On the upper level, the fully-realized solar principle operates as the influx of superconscious life and wisdom that brings light and life into the personal form.

☾ The Lunar Principle

The Moon represents the light of subconscious connection and power. The word subconscious in reference to the lunar principle does not indicate that it is less important than the solar principle, but rather that it operates in a way inaccessible to the mind. In other words, it functions under the radar of self-conscious observation, though it may be influenced and directed through concentrated thought.

The solar and lunar principles are both emanations of the same light that has taken different forms. When light is in lunar form, it operates as the connective power upon which all sentient life rests.

Like the solar principle, in AstroYoga the lunar principle is twofold. There is the impersonal light of the actual Moon, representing the light of subconscious awareness that is the connective force among and through all beings. There is also the personal subconscious factor, as seen in the natal chart. Both of these lunar tendencies can be worked with in your AstroYoga practice. The lunar principle can be integrated into the body to heighten your directive influence over both your emotional nature and your connection to all beings.

The personal lunar principle represents the very force that allows the human body to stay alive without any self-conscious input. It's this principle that keeps your cells working, lungs breathing, heart beating, and body alive while you sleep. It's also this principle that works out answers to life's most interesting questions in the layer of consciousness beneath the mind, as well as forms the emotional and personal bonds we have with others. On a fundamental level, the lunar principle is the intelligence that takes place below the conscious awareness of the mind. The mechanisms by which the lunar principle operates are not understood by the conscious mind. However, its operational laws may be understood; the subconscious principle always responds to suggestion and operates through principles of elaboration, rhythm, and memory.

It is your personal lunar principle that connects you to others, creates intentional and unintentional manifestations, alerts you to danger or safety via your intuition, and nurtures you to build your overall health.

Something of note is that the lunar principle is what manifestation exercises are primarily concerned with, although few people articulate these techniques as such. Many people seek to manifest with the new moon, and do not see why. Manifesting with the Moon is a practice because the lunar principle is the form of consciousness that connects you with whom and what you are destined to interact. If your desire is true and you rightly influence the lunar principle present within you, success is inevitable.

> **A word of caution:** Before proceeding to draw conclusions within AstroYoga, it is essential that you ground yourself in right understanding and principles of truth. This is essential because the lunar consciousness will elaborate the feelings, beliefs, and reasonings impressed upon it, reflecting its nature back to you several times over. Therefore, always consciously employ your powers of observation, reasoning, and positive intention so that the influence upon your subconscious may be favorable. Suggest to your lunar principle that you expect alignment with truth, harmony, peace, and love, and watch it unfold in your life many times over.
>
> In yogic texts such as Patanjali's *Yoga Sutras*, a central tenant of yoga is ishvara pranidhana, usually translated as surrender to God or to the higher Self. In a world with so many approaches to consciousness, spirituality, and religions, ishvara pranidhana is often misunderstood, yet it is of the utmost importance in yoga.
>
> The lunar consciousness elaborates whatever is impressed upon it. When the self-consciousness has a misunderstanding or is influenced by past negative experience, then the subconscious will be influenced negatively. However, when you invite your highest self into your reasoning and take higher perspectives on life, then the lunar subconscious is influenced positively. This creates success in your life, manifestations, and desires.
>
> The lunar subconscious has direct access to the higher forms of the solar superconsciousness and is also influenced by the self-conscious. You always have free will, and so the lunar principle will operate according to your predominating suggestion to it. If you practice surrendering to the highest good and to your highest form of Self, then the lunar principle will operate in harmony with your own highest good.

Sadly, many people dismiss lunar understandings without an eye for the many planes of existence on which this principle is at play, treating it more like a fairy godmother than an integrative essential piece of the self and of the reality of consciousness.

Just like the visible Moon in the sky, the lunar principle in an individual person is changeable, going through phases from new to full and back again, and creating waves of emotion and sensation inside and around that person.

Through the sea of shifting emotional states, the moon works to build reality to align with the predominating mental and emotional states of an individual. To fully integrate the moon means to live life in such a way that all changing emotional states may be reconciled back to the individual's predominating state of consciousness. In other words, emotions are not viewed as the drivers behind life, but are viewed as sign posts to alert you to changing conditions to be addressed or weathered. No state is shunned, but rather the individual self-nurtures back to a state of personal equilibrium. This personal equilibrium creates the predominating state that influences principles of manifestation and physical wellbeing in a person's life.

The lunar principle reminds us that each person has the power to shift this state of equilibrium. A generally lack-luster existence may be made delightful, or a generally optimistic person may be made sullen. The predominating state arises through the field of time.

Layers of Light Made Manifest

We've established that the solar and lunar principles are at play on all levels of conscious existence. Serious students of AstroYoga may recall that there are levels of reality in which the solar and lunar principles are not separated, such as what is termed the Hridaya—the great heart in which the dance of polarity ceases to exist because there is no-thing beyond it. But even then, we do not know how the solar and lunar principles operate beyond the ati ati suksma, the extremely subtle layers of reality. Now let's examine a few layers of reality upon which the solar and lunar principles operate as they relate to AstroYoga.

Physical and Chemical Shifts

One notable way the solar and lunar principles are at play in yoga is through physical and chemical shifts in the body. There are certain solar and lunar centers in the brain that remain dormant or are only partially activated until brought to life through physiological shifts facilitated through such practices as pranayama and meditation. These shifts are whole-body events, generally starting with the body's response to air and food in a new way. Through self-conscious practice aligning with the solar principle and subconscious lunar integration, the body begins to react to the same stimuli in different ways. This results in better nutrient absorption, a shift in the chemical makeup of the blood, and an awakening of higher areas of consciousness that can be accessed through the physical structures in the brain.

There are other notable physical shifts that can occur as well, and these often present themselves before the phenomena mentioned above. These can include: shifts in muscle tone; the expression or dormancy of specific traits; the expression or dormancy of disease; the nature of nervous system response; and shifts in physical appearance. These changes all wind up relating to the main physiological shift discussed above. In many instances, health on all levels is directly accessible through our relationship with our own consciousness.

Nadis and Energetic Shifts

The solar and lunar principles are related to the nadis, or energetic channels in the body. Though there are many nadis in the physical form, there are three primary nadis that intertwine with the chakra system of the yogic energy body.

Pingala and Ida nadis are two of the primary channels in the body. Pingala nadi is the solar nadi which originates at the base of the spine in the muladhara (root) chakra and weaves through the chakras until winding up at the right nostril. Ida nadi also originates in muladhara and weaves through the chakras, taking a complementary path and ending in the left nostril.

The third of the primary nadis is known as Sushumna nadi. This is the central channel that moves straight up from muladhara chakra to and through the point known as sahasrara, the mystical point of the seventh chakra located at the crown, which represents access to the higher consciousnesses available to awakened humanity.

Sushumna nadi may be viewed as the unification of the two luminary forces. When the solar and lunar principles unite in the human body, a powerful form of consciousness known as kundalini arises through these nadis, which results in awakening certain potencies in the chakras, brain centers, and physical body.

In the uniting of Ida and Pingala nadis, there is an important truth: all pairs of supposed opposites can be reconciled, and paradoxes only seem as such at certain levels of awareness. Though it is necessary in this life to grapple with the opposing forces and paradoxes that arise in the lived expression of existence, it's also helpful to adopt the perspective that all in all, opposites within us must unite in order to reach certain stages of human development.

To clear and energize the nadis is the work of pranayama. Practicing specific pranayama exercises exact particular, predictable results on the nadis and energy body. These in turn create shifts in the physical and outer world as well. If you are in doubt of which pranayama exercises are appropriate for your particular aims, practice nadi shodhana (alternate nostril breath) and ujjayi pranayama (victoriously uprising breath), as they build energy and balance the nadis while being safe for anyone.

External Shifts

Properly working with the solar and lunar principles will have resonant effects outside the physical body. Each shift that takes place within you simultaneously activates additional harmonically aligned shifts outside of you.

The solar principle is what allows you to see more clearly. This is true physically with eyesight, but it is also true that you will be able to see more clearly into situations and patterns of cause and effect around you. Seeing these patterns in nature and culture will help you to understand the operations of reality, including physics, metaphysics, and manifestation. When you have this clarity in your mind and heart, you'll find the world reveals itself to you in ways that make it easier to navigate.

The lunar principle is what allows you to build the material world as you see fit. You'll see that people, resources, and influences come into your life in the proper moments, and that your external reality begins to reflect your inner state. This does not mean that you will avoid all unfortunate encounters, but rather that the majority of immediate, external events begin to show themselves to you in terms of your own inner state of awareness. Because your state has shifted, you notice different options, and respond with greater freedom. Inner and outer states relate. Use the lunar principle to create with the awareness that develops within.

As things shift within you, the world reflects itself back to you in many ways. You may even begin to see more clearly the influence your inner state has on the world outside of you, as well as how your inner state and the inner world of others co-create the realm in which we all live.

Chapter 3: An Energetic Understanding of the Zodiac

Key Points in this Chapter
- The zodiac is a circle that can be subdivided several ways to demonstrate how the signs relate to one another.
- The zodiac may be examined according to gender, mode of expression (cardinal, fixed, mutable), or element (fire, air, water, earth).
- Approaching the zodiac through an understanding of its subdivisions is a useful approach before diving deeply into the energetic contemplation of any one sign.

The Zodiac is One and Many

The zodiac is the piece of astrology that people typically are most familiar with. Although the zodiac signs are familiar to the general public, within them are many secrets that will become common knowledge in the Aquarian Age to come.

While it is beyond the scope of this book to go into every detail about each sign, I'll present a framework which can serve as a starting point for deeper contemplation and further research.

If you've been waiting for a message that it's time to go beyond memorizing lists of associations with the zodiac signs, this is it! Although it's useful to know the associated meanings with signs (and planets too, when we get to that), it's necessary to integrate understanding beyond lists and charts. When you have an integrated understanding of the zodiac, this symbolic language becomes active in your subconscious and conscious mind as a way to build, transmute, and discern reality.

The word zodiac means a circle of animals. This word comes from the Latin zodiacus and the Greek zodiakos kuklos. Here you can see the root word for circle (kuklos), and the root for animals, which is the same root for zoo and zoology that we have in modern English. In this etymology we find a truth that the zodiac is singular, as in the entire circle, and also many, since the animals indicated are plural. The circular nature of the zodiac also implies that geometry is intrinsic to astrology, and by association number and numerology.

This connection to number and geometry is a clue that's left to modern practitioners from ancient linguistics. It's beyond the scope of this book to fully explore numerology, but a working grasp of the subject will be helpful as you delve further into AstroYoga. For right now, suffice it to say that in symbolic systems, numbers signify specific meanings beyond quantity and measure. You can begin to work with them when you understand how they have been encoded, used, and interpreted, as well as how they show up in the natural world in physics, astronomy, music, and geometry. A curiosity about number and language is quite useful when exploring the synchronicities present in your AstroYoga practice.

One: The Zodiac as a Single Circle

The zodiac is first and foremost a circle. It's worth noting that the circle implies both zero and one, since the circle is both a single definite shape, and also the symbol of the number zero.

In AstroYoga, zero refers to the absolute principle of reality, sometimes symbolized as the egg of space in esoteric yoga and astrology. This egg represents the container for all life that at once encompasses and permeates all beings in their manifest and potential forms. This reference is connected to the life breath, or prana, which is the essence from which all life is created and sustained.

The circle is also singular, which brings up symbolism surrounding the number one. One signifies concepts such as concentration, direction of personal power, beginnings, specification, and definition. Furthermore, when the number one is present, it always implies the presence of more; if you have one of anything, it is defined as separate from what it is not. So to have any one thing, there must necessarily be something else from which it is set apart. Even the shape of the numeral one implies this. When you draw the numeral for the number one, it's a line segment; geometrically this is the connection between two points.

The zodiac exists as an energetic continuum that spans the range of human experience and personality, existing within the cyclic realm of time. Since everyone's chart is a depiction of the zodiac itself, the zodiac also implies ideas about the nature of humanity. The zodiac's definite form suggests the definite shape of human personality, while its circular nature serves as a reminder that every human being is inherently whole, when we take a higher perspective. This is just one of many symbolic depictions of humanity that examines the intertwined relationship between the physical and the spiritual.

Two: The Zodiac as Masculine and Feminine

In yoga philosophy there are conceptual layers of reality called tattvas. The tattva model examines aspects of conscious experience in various layers of reality. In the tattva structure of reality from non-dual Shaivism, 36 tattvas are enumerated, adding to the 25 tattvas of other schools. The top tattva is the great heart, or Hrydaya, which indicates the wholeness of all reality. From the Hrydaya comes the masculine-encoded Shiva and feminine-encoded Shakti, or the higher harmonic potencies of the forms of awareness represented by the Sun and Moon, respectively. Likewise, from the circle of the zodiac representing wholeness, the zodiac splits into two parts, each encoded according to gender.

> When reading forms of sidereal astrology from India, the chart is generally laid out as a square. The zodiac is a circle, but the boxed shape has other indications. Though sidereal charts are often square simply for ease of drawing, the shape points toward other ends for students of symbol.
>
> That the zodiac can be drawn as a circle or a square warrants a discussion on the ancient mystery of 'squaring the circle,' a mathematical conundrum seeking to find a way to draw a circle and a square that contain the same area. This was thought to be mathematically impossible due to the nature of pi (π), a number essential for calculations connected to circles. Interestingly, the shape of the square was thought to be symbolic of manifest reality and form, while the circle was considered a depiction of the cosmic, spiritual forces. Some philosophers took this mathematical question as symbolic of the relationship between the material and the spiritual.
>
> Squaring the circle is a mathematical quandary that puzzled mathematicians for the longest time—the most famous answer to which is found in DaVinci's Vitruvian Man, in which he demonstrated that the space to fill both a circle and a square could be found in the human form. Indeed, the space needed to fill both a circle and a square can also be found in the cosmic form of human personality: the zodiac.

Remember that while you may have a personal gender expression on the external plane, you are a whole being on the internal plane. Gender in AstroYoga refers to a particular energetic spectrum which implies the patterns of behavior within your own consciousness.

The Tattvas			
The Hridaya (Heart), Perfect Unison			
Shiva (God Potency, Consciousness)		Shakti (Goddess Potency, Power)	
Sadashiva (Pure Universe, Compassion): Iccha (Willing)			
Ishvara (Pure Divinity): Jnana (Knowing)			
Shuddha-Vidya (Pure Mantra): Kriya (Acting)			
Maya (The Power of Differentiation)			
Kala (Differentiated Agency)			
Vidya (Differentiated Knowledge)			
Raga (Desire)			
Kala (Time)			
Niyati (Binding to Karma and Place)			
Purusha (Individual Consciousness)		Prakriti (Primordial Nature)	
Buddhi (Discernment)			
Ahamkara ('I' Construct or Ego)			
Manas (Mental Attention and Sense Awareness)			
Sense Capacities	Action Capacities	Subtle Elements	Great Elements
Ears	Speaking	Sound	Space
Skin	Grasping	Touch	Wind
Eyes	Ambulating	Appearance	Fire
Tongue	Procreating	Flavor	Water
Nose	Eliminating	Odor	Earth

Just because you have prominent astrology placements in signs of a particular gender does not mean that you will necessarily self-express as that gender. What gender does imply in these systems is whether the primary field of influence is in the subconscious or self-conscious layers of your own internal state.

The masculine signs in the zodiac are: Aries, Gemini, Leo, Libra, Sagittarius, and Aquarius.

The feminine signs in the zodiac are: Taurus, Cancer, Virgo, Scorpio, Capricorn, and Pisces.

Generally speaking, the masculine signs are primarily concerned with aspects of consciousness that act upon desire, either through the body (Aries, Leo, and Sagittarius) or through the mind (Gemini, Libra, and Aquarius). The feminine signs are primarily concerned with magnetizing the desire-force either through the imagination/intuition (Cancer, Scorpio, and Pisces) or through the physical plane (Taurus, Virgo, and Capricorn).

It's important to reflect on these natures first and foremost as aspects of yourself. When a clear picture of these energies is understood, these energies manifesting in the external plane will give you additional information to aid in deepening your relationship with yourself and the zodiac as it exists in you.

Three: The Zodiac as Modes of Motion

The zodiac signs have three ways in which they move energy. These are known as the quadruplicities or modalities.

Occasionally, I receive questions about the word quadruplicity. Astrology students often question why there are three quadruplicities, since the root 'quad' implies four. Even though there are three groups of quadruplicities, each group contains four zodiac signs. The quadruplicities of the zodiac are cardinal, fixed, and mutable. Each of these modalities occurs in each of the four zodiac elements. This means each quadruplicity is associated with a single fire, water, air, and earth sign.

Cardinal signs move directionally from one point to another. The element through which they move determines what they are moving toward. The cardinal signs are Aries, Cancer, Libra, and Capricorn.

Fixed signs sustain, gather, and hold energy. Their element determines what they hold and consider to be worthy of value and attention. The fixed signs are Taurus, Leo, Scorpio, and Aquarius.

Mutable signs circulate, change, and dissolve energy. What they are shifting is determined by their element. The mutable signs are Gemini, Virgo, Sagittarius, and Pisces.

When contemplating the quadruplicities, it is essential to consider how energy moves in general. If you're not already aware of what sort of movement predominates the various functions of your inner state and outer actions, give this due consideration to get a strong hint as to which zodiac energies are most prevalent for you.

	Fire	Air	Water	Earth
Cardinal	Aries	Libra	Cancer	Capricorn
Fixed	Leo	Aquarius	Scorpio	Taurus
Mutable	Sagittarius	Gemini	Pisces	Virgo

Four: The Zodiac as Elements

The zodiac has four standard elements associated with the signs. They are fire, air, water, and earth. These are also called the triplicities, due to the fact that there are three signs of each element, each of a different modality.

The element of a zodiac sign determines the energetic substance that is influenced by that sign. Where the quadruplicity defines the manner in which a zodiac sign moves, the triplicity/element defines the field through which a zodiac sign moves. Through the combination of quadruplicity and triplicity, each zodiac sign has its domain which is distinct from all other signs. By understanding these elements and how they manifest in the body, you'll have a strong foundation for much of what AstroYoga has to offer. To break down elements more fully in terms of the energy body, read the section in chapter six on the koshas, or energetic sheaths of the subtle body.

△ **The Fire Signs are Aries, Leo, and Sagittarius.**

Fire represents the spark of life, the flame of creativity, and spirit, which is the life breath of any human soul. There is fire within you, and if you can align with the fire signs, you can harness their power in your life. There is fire in: the creativity of the heart; the movement of the muscles; and the impulses that arise within you that urge you to move like Aries, express like Leo, or seek like Sagittarius.

You can get in touch with the fire element by noticing it in your body. Can you see the light in your eyes when you gaze in the mirror? What is that flame saying to you? Do you sense the burning of desire when you feel a craving for sensual experience? What sensations arise in you when anger is present? Where is the origin of the urge to move your body to walk forward, work, or play? What is the force at play in your digestion of both food and experiences?

The Air Signs are Gemini, Libra, and Aquarius.

Air represents thought and mental clarity. The air that's within you is more than the atmospheric air that you breathe. You may notice air in the swiftness of thought, the translation of thought to other forms in the body through the nervous system, and the quality of breath and the breath's circulation through the blood. There is air in: the associative nature of the hands and nervous system; the balancing and regulation of the blood; the movement of the breath; and the awareness that arises when you associate like Gemini, respond like Libra, and innovate like Aquarius.

You can get in touch with the air element by noticing it in your body. Can you stay aware of your breath while doing other activities? What are the form and quality of your thoughts? In what ways do you react to surprise? In what ways does your breath or quality of circulation affect your thoughts?

The Water Signs are Cancer, Scorpio, and Pisces.

Water represents the emotions, intuition, and etherial substance of memory and potentiality. Even though we are made of about 70 percent water, the water in astrology refers both to physical water and to etheric water that makes up the subconscious, imaginative, intuitive mind-stuff. There is water in the blood, lymph, sexual fluids, digestive fluids, cerebral-spinal fluid, breasts, and brain. There is also water in imagination and in all intelligences within you that rely on impression, elaboration, and duplication of experience. It's water that allows you to nurture like Cancer, hold your power like Scorpio, or allow the flow of intuition like Pisces. These are not entirely separate from the physical manifestations of water within you.

You can get in touch with the water element by noticing it in your body. Where are you most fluid, and what intelligences are to be found there? When you imagine your desires, where do these images originate in your body-mind? When you still yourself for meditation, can you feel the subtle spanda pulsation moving through your form? What are you feeling now?

> Spanda in Sanskrit refers to the pulsation of the life force. This subtle sensation can be felt at any time if you still yourself and wait.

The Earth Signs are Taurus, Virgo, and Capricorn.

Earth represents what is manifest: the practical tools and forms that surround you. Technically, earth is a mixture of the other elements, and while it is the most apparent element to our senses because of its tangibility, it potentially is also the most illusory, since it must be looked into in order to reveal its true nature. The earth element is present in anything tangible, and therefore this element is present in the fullness of your physical form. There's earth in your bones, joints, structural form, and assimilation of the raw materials in digestion. There's also earth in your wellbeing, habitual patterns, and hygiene, as well as when you sustain yourself like Taurus, organize your body like Virgo, and direct your physical energies like Capricorn.

> **Note:** A great deal of attention should be given to the elements in your studies. While at first glance they may appear to be separate from one another, a careful consideration will reveal many important truths about the relationship between air, fire, water, earth, and the totality of life.

You can get in touch with the earth element by noticing the entirety of your physical experience. What do you sense as the intelligence in your bones? What physically gives your body structure and form, and how is that an aspect of your own awareness? What tightness, soreness, or twinges are present, and what messages are they offering you? What physical boons do you have at your disposal? What do you love and appreciate about your body? In what ways do you habitually care for your body?

Six: The Zodiac as Pairs of Opposites

Every sign has an opposite in the zodiac wheel. The zodiac has six energetic continuums, or pairs of signs. They are zodiac opposites, and opposites imply similar substance at different places along a vibratory spectrum. In the same way that hot and cold are both temperature (that is, the vibration of matter creating cold, hot, or tepid sensation), the pairs of zodiac signs define themselves according to where they fall in their particular spectrum of expression.

Note: Astrology has a Northern Hemisphere bias. This is due to the fact that most of the world's land mass is in the Northern Hemisphere, and also because astrology and yoga developed primarily in the Northern Hemisphere in the hubs of the ancient world. This concept of energetic continuum is happening on the Earth as well as in the chart. Quite literally with the seasons, when one of these zodiac signs is awakened, its opposite climate is also happening somewhere else in the world. Use an understanding of the energetic continuums of the zodiac to make accurate impressions when reading charts for the Southern Hemisphere (either for birth location, relocation, or for the present location of the person).

The Aries-Libra spectrum is the continuum of self to relationship, as well as action to the outcome of actions as they impact yourself and others. It's one of two Mars-Venus spectrums in the zodiac. Along this spectrum we determine how much of ourselves to pour into relationships, as well as what is fair when examining personal expression verses deference toward others. This spectrum can teach how to use the personal action principle in the service of love.

The Taurus-Scorpio spectrum is the continuum of what is manifest to what exists in potential form. It's the second of two Mars-Venus spectrums in the zodiac. Along this spectrum we embody the dual nature of the cycles of life, death, birth, rebirth, and change. This spectrum can teach how to recognize love as possibility, as manifest forms, and as the principle of change itself.

The Gemini-Sagittarius spectrum is the continuum of familiar knowledge, people, and places to broader exploration of high ideals, far places, and people who expand our sense of what's possible. It's one of two Mercury-Jupiter spectrums in the zodiac. Along this spectrum we form opinions and beliefs through familiarity and broader exploration. This spectrum teaches how we know what we know, and it can support or hinder a quest for true knowledge, depending on your approach.

The Cancer-Capricorn spectrum is the continuum of nurture to work. It's one of two Luminary-Saturn spectrums in the zodiac. Along this spectrum we balance discretion and emotion, as well as effort with nurture. This spectrum can teach the right connection to your subconsciousness in terms of personal, systematic influence and the nourishing support of your body and intuition.

The Leo-Aquarius spectrum is the continuum of self-rulership to community. It's the second of two Luminary-Saturn spectrums in the zodiac. Along this spectrum we learn how to shine brightly while in an embodied reality, as well as how to balance the personal sovereignty of the self with the necessity to connect with others in community. This spectrum can teach how the enlightened self shines most brightly when applied to structure and form.

The Virgo-Pisces spectrum is the continuum of order to entropy. It's the second of two Mercury-Jupiter spectrums in the zodiac. Along this spectrum we learn how to strike the balance between controlling and allowing, as well as categorizing and mixing things together. This spectrum can teach how to use the mind to expand your spiritual life.

Twelve and More: The Zodiac Signs and Their Subdivisions

The most well-known categorization of the zodiac is by sign, of which there are twelve. In chapters five and six, you'll learn more about the zodiac signs, their associations with the body, the energies they represent, and how they connect with yoga.

The subdivisions of the single circle don't stop at twelve. Each zodiac sign is subdivided into three decans of ten degrees each for a division of 36. You can think of the decans as the beginning, middle, and end of a sign.

Beyond the decans, the circle is divided into 360 degrees. This is significant because each degree of the zodiac has a subtle distinction from every other degree in the zodiac. Clearly understanding each degree in the zodiac and how it relates to the body is helpful to make the work you do with AstroYoga the most accurate it can be.

There are secrets hidden in the zodiac, the keys to which are written in language, culture, folklore, spiritual texts, and yoga. The more you work with the zodiac, the more intensely and intimately you'll glean these secrets both from your practices and the world around you.

Zodiac Energetics

Zodiac Sign	Gender	Modality	Element	Polarity
Aries	Masculine	Cardinal	Fire	Libra
Taurus	Feminine	Fixed	Earth	Scorpio
Gemini	Masculine	Mutable	Air	Sagittarius
Cancer	Feminine	Cardinal	Water	Capricorn
Leo	Masculine	Fixed	Fire	Aquarius
Virgo	Feminine	Mutable	Earth	Pisces
Libra	Masculine	Cardinal	Air	Aries
Scorpio	Feminine	Fixed	Water	Taurus
Sagittarius	Masculine	Mutable	Fire	Gemini
Capricorn	Feminine	Cardinal	Earth	Cancer
Aquarius	Masculine	Fixed	Air	Leo
Pisces	Feminine	Mutable	Water	Virgo

Chapter 4: Who Are the Planets?

Key Points in this Chapter
- The planets are the personified actors of the zodiac.
- Each planet has a glyph made from circles, crescents, and crosses. These glyphs symbolize the planetary characteristics.
- Each planet has a zodiac home, or domicile, and some planets have signs of exaltation, where they are most celebrated.
- Learning to work with the planets is essential to activating positive outcomes in your AstroYoga practice.

The Active Principles of AstroYoga

In astrology, yoga, and your body, the planets are the active principles of the zodiac. These planets are personified as beings who are the actors against the backdrop of the zodiac's energetic arenas.

Traditionally, the planets have been referred to as deities. As you work with them and take measure of your life through working with their principles, you are welcome to consider them in a way that is comfortable for you. Take the time to learn and assign the symbolism that has been passed down for thousands of years about the planets.

Additionally, it is helpful to connect the planets to their different personalities and view them as actors in your psyche, body, and world. Some overlook the wisdom of traditional knowledge, but as students of AstroYoga we look to the hidden truths presented in these traditions. Jung's famous archetypical language is also helpful in this subject, as he asserts there are personal aspects of universal themes abiding in each one of us.

It's easy to see why these ancient systems considered the planets as deities, since life tends to go much more smoothly the more you operate in harmony with the planets, and reality tends to operate in accordance with their patterns.

To be clear, I am not suggesting that you write off responsibility for your life, resign yourself to a fear-based approach of difficult transits, or decide that you're at the mercy of something like fate. Rather, I'm suggesting you take into account that each of these planetary forces operates as an actual, physical reality in your body and the world. Taking the planets into consideration helps you align your perceptions with truth.

When you align your perceptions with truth as described by the planets, two things happen. First, you realize that reality is reflecting your inner world back to you, even if it comes with challenges to overcome. Second, you make yourself more likely to succeed in creating your preferred future, because you've taken an accurate assessment of yourself and the character of the present moment.

Understand that the planets represent aspects of you. In various moments your body, spirit, and psyche express these planetary forces in various combinations. Learning to recognize the planets' work in your life is an important step in connecting AstroYoga to your desires and life circumstances.

The Circle, Crescent, and Cross: The Symbols in Planetary Glyphs

When looking at the planets, it's essential to recognize what the symbols for each planet represent. Each planetary glyph is made up entirely of the circle, crescent, cross, or a combination of these symbols. The manner in which these symbols are arranged indicates something significant about how a particular planet operates.

The Circle:

The circle is related to the solar principle discussed in chapter two. In astrology, anytime you're dealing with a circle, you're connecting with forces that tap into the superconscious principle of reality. In other words, circles represent the light of awareness connected with the Sun and higher principles of cosmic intelligence. The circle represents the light given from your higher self. Yet in practice, the circle may also symbolize an ego construct of what you mistakenly presume to be your higher self. When a circle is present in a glyph, it shows the placement of the light of your spirit as the operating principle in that glyph. The placements of circles in planetary glyphs and in charts show arenas where it's best to align yourself with your highest level of consciousness.

The Crescent:

The crescent is related to the lunar principle discussed in chapter two. In astrology, anytime you're dealing with a crescent, you're connecting with forces that tap into the subconscious principle of reality. This is what both builds reality as it constantly unfolds and taps into the perfect memory of the universe known as the akashic record. When a crescent is present in a glyph, it shows the manner and direction in which the subconscious operates. Because the subconscious principle is always at play and operates according to suggestion, the influence and receptivity of the subconscious nature as symbolized by the crescent can operate in various ways per planet.

The Cross:

The cross is related to the earth principle of manifest reality and self-consciousness. Self-consciousness is the level of awareness that registers energies, objects, and people through the thinking, feeling, and sensing mind. In astrology, anytime you're dealing with a cross, arrow, or X (all variations of a cross), you're connecting with a principle of what exists in manifest reality. People often say that 'X marks the spot' when referring to treasure maps because treasure is something tangible and able to be found in a definite location. When a cross appears in a glyph, it shows the manner in which self-conscious awareness and tangible reality operate. Both self-conscious awareness and tangible reality can be sustained, directed, or utilized, according to what forces are at play in the involved planets.

A Word on Rulership and Exaltation

It's necessary to understand how the zodiac and planets relate to one another. A deeper contemplation of each zodiac sign is coming in the next chapter, but for now suffice it to say that each planet has a zodiac sign where it is most at home, as well as a sign where it is most celebrated.

I like to use the analogy of going to your own home verses heading to a favorite relative's house. When you walk in your home, there's a comfortable feeling where routines take place and you can refresh yourself. But, when you visit your favorite relative's house, it feels like a special occasion where you're a celebrated guest.

Likewise, planets in their zodiac homes (or domiciles) are abiding in their natural state of being. Things feel at ease in that sign, much like your home may seem to you. When planets enter their sign of exaltation, much like visiting your favorite relative in the example above, they begin to express the highest potency that particular planet has to offer. As you move through this book, keep this idea in mind, and consider how it plays out in your body, your chart, and your life.

Planetary Rulership and Exaltation

Planet	Sign of Rulership	Sign of Exaltation
Sun	Leo	Aries
Moon	Cancer	Taurus
Mercury	Gemini, Virgo	Virgo
Venus	Taurus, Libra	Pisces
Mars	Aries, Scorpio	Capricorn
Jupiter	Sagittarius, Pisces	Cancer
Saturn	Capricorn, Aquarius	Libra

The Sun and the Moon

The Sun and the Moon were discussed in chapter two, but since in astrology they are considered planets, I'll mention them here as well. The word planet refers to any planet, object, or luminary that we are examining in the birth chart, although you're welcome to be more specific in your vocabulary when differentiating types of objects in more advanced studies.

As a reminder, when discussing zodiac seasons in relationship to the planets, I am defaulting to tropical time. Remember that sidereal time is always simultaneously occurring as an overtone to the tropical seasons.

The Sun is most at home in Leo and is exalted in Aries. Leo season takes place in the heart of summer, when the Sun is strongest and most powerful, and Aries season initiates at the vernal equinox, when the Sun is returning to the North to bring springtime. The solar principle represents the light of awareness. While Leo season embodies the full power of the conscious principle, Aries season brings the promise of expanding consciousness as connected to the emerging forms of life in springtime.

The Moon is most at home in Cancer and is exalted in Taurus. Cancer season takes place during the initial phase of summer when summer berries and summer flowers are flourishing, and Taurus season takes place in the heart of spring when the flowering trees and early flowers are at their peak. These blossoming times echo the subconscious promise that lunar intelligence is working under the surface at all times for things to be made manifest in due course.

As you consider the Sun, the Moon, and other planets, keep in mind that rulership and exaltation describe cosmic influences that can transform the experience of the physical and subtle body. When considered carefully, these rulerships and exaltations create a map to the unfolding, interconnected reality of your physical and subtle forms. The relationship among the Sun, Moon, and nadis of the body were discussed in chapter two, but as you read the next few chapters, you'll discover that rulerships, exaltations, and planetary tendencies connect to each layer of your being. These concepts are primary keys in unlocking the character of time and development of the physical and subtle body through AstroYoga.

Mercury

Mercury is the only planet without a specifically-defined gender.

When considering the Sun and Moon, we discover that gender in astrology and yoga is used to show particular modalities of consciousness—the pure, disembodied consciousness (solar/masculine) and the embodied principle of power and manifestation (lunar/feminine). Mercury contains aspects of both, as it is both the mind and the messenger.

Of course, it doesn't take long to realize that every human is composed of the solar-lunar principles, and that while we may have an externally embodied gender, the totality of these spectrums is available to each of us.

This is where Mercury comes in. Mercury puts forth the idea that the human mind has no gender in and of itself. Furthermore, Mercury also asserts that the human mind is the messenger that helps us receive and translate communication from higher planes of awareness.

Linguistically and practically, Mercury deals with the mind. Let's break down some words to see how the mind reflects back to the symbolism of Mercury. In Sanskrit one word for the mind is manas. Manas etymologically traces to the English words man, woman, and human. It also links to the word for hands in many Romance languages, as in the Spanish manos.

These linguistic connections to Mercury are significant because the first sign that Mercury rules is Gemini, which is related to both the mind and the hands, as well as the smaller-self ideas we use to form personality-specific perceptions of the world. Also, the word manas specifically tracks across the solar and lunar principles since it describes both the mind and the intelligence of the body.

Looking at this from a different angle to gain more perspective, the Sanskrit name for the planet Mercury is Buddhi, which is another aspect of the mind. This part of the mind is more rational with a higher potential to see truth. This is tied to the fact that the second sign Mercury rules (Virgo) is a link between the physical and the mental. Virgo is also the sign of Mercury's exaltation.

AstroYoga teaches that success in its practice occurs when mere perception is set aside for rational truth that harmonizes with the real form of the body. Virgo plays a key role here, since mental and physical attunement relate directly to a high vibration of Virgo. Virgo relates to health, as well as the highest forms of rational thought, which we'll discuss more in the next chapter.

In mythology, Mercury is the messenger of the gods, and is sometimes referred to as Hermes, Hermes Trismegistus, or Thoth. Legend holds that the being known as Thoth, or Hermes, was the first human to master and teach astrology and the other metaphysical arts from which modern astrology and yoga have taken form. Etymologically, the English word thought comes from Thoth. In legend, Thoth is immortalized among the stars, having raised his human vibration to something in harmony with divinity.

In this legend is another clue, which is an undercurrent of all AstroYoga practice. Namely: the body is given to us as a tool for discovering the Great Mystery, which is in essence an understanding and mastery of consciousness on many levels, though words do not do it justice since the Great Mystery cannot be fully described in language. As we work with the body and mind, we have the opportunity to raise ourselves to a point of vibrational harmony that aligns life on Earth with that of a heavenly and harmonious state.

The symbol for Mercury is a caduceus. This is the staff carried by Mercury, which is depicted with two intertwined snakes leading to a pair of wings at the top. As we'll discuss more fully later in the book, this is a symbolic depiction of what happens when the kundalini force rises though the nadis, with Ida and Pingala coalescing in Sushumna, eventually piercing the ajna, third-eye space, in the center of the brow.

The glyph depicts a crescent atop a circle atop a cross. This glyph looks like a caduceus and points to what happens when Mercury is operating at a high level. When used well, Mercury teaches how to raise the subconscious to create the reality of the superconscious in every aspect of your life. As well, it teaches how to use the mind to create a future to your liking.

Alchemy: There is a nearly universal dictum that even enlightened beings should study the ancient teachings. Not only does studying Mercury's powers echo this dictum, but these concepts also help to decode the old alchemical maxim that Mercury can turn your matter to gold.

Modern thinking occasionally derides alchemy for believing that it could change lead into gold through the agency of Mercury. To modern thinkers, this may appear as an impossibility. Yet, like many ancient wisdom traditions, the alchemists had to encode their meditation practices to protect them from the culture of enforced orthodoxy surrounding them in their time.

In alchemy, Mercury shows up in two primary locations. First, Mercury arises as one of the triad of mercury, sulpher, and salt, which roughly correspond to the three gunas in yoga, or strands that weave together to form reality: mercury to sattva; sulpher to rajas; and salt to tamas. Second, Mercury shows up as quicksilver, one of the seven metals representing the seven original planets. Lead corresponds to Saturn and the boundaries of the manifest world in time and space. The Sun corresponds to gold. So Mercury represents the principle or agent of change, which allows the manifest world to become infused with solar consciousness.

For reference, here is a list of the metals of alchemy: Saturn as lead; Jupiter as tin; Mars as iron; Venus as copper; Mercury as quicksilver; the Moon as silver; and the Sun as gold.

♀ Venus

Venus is well-known as the goddess of beauty, desire, and love. In AstroYoga, Venus energy is a central power coalescing abundance, love, good taste, and beauty. Sayings about love and beauty persist in culture, yet they are often used to the point of being cliché. Sayings such as 'beauty is the reason,' 'beauty needs no reason,' and 'love is all there is,' all hint at the primary importance of Venus energy. Far from the faddist depiction of commercialized fashion and beauty, Venusian beauty loves, nourishes, expresses health and wellbeing, and creates a sense of true contentment and enjoyment in life.

In mythology, stories of Venus, Aphrodite, and Lakshmi abound with these Venusian goddesses simply leaving the scene if they are insulted or attacked. When Venus leaves, beauty vanishes, health is destroyed, and life feels positively depressing. The very beings who offended her usually beg her to return, once they see how they starve and suffer without her presence. Venus energy is something essential for life, and yet, the truth in these old tales is that many of us take her for granted. Health is often ignored until it's gone; abundance is flaunted and spent until times of austerity; and those we love (including ourselves) are so easily taken for granted.

To use Venus energy well means to both embody and appreciate her, before you offend her delicate sensibilities and she leaves you for someone who gives her due credit. Venus energy is that which you cherish, desire, hold to be dear, and use as an expression of love or aesthetics. This is true both in yourself and in the world around you.

Venus vibrates with the energy of the Earth. This is indicated by the first sign she rules, Taurus, the fixed sign of the earth element. Earth freely gives to us and with more abundance than we could ever ask. Earth's gifts are intensified when we treat her well, tend our gardens, and enter into a state of harmony with her.

The second sign Venus rules is Libra, an air sign whose primary purposes are partnership and the law of karma (action and reaction). Venus' rulership of these themes exemplifies that we best respond to things when we are acting in love and with integrity toward those things we desire, especially when considering other beings.

Venus' exaltation is in Pisces, whose primary vibration is one of releasing control and dissolving into oneness with the universe. This shares an important truth that love is all there is, as the old saying goes. When we let go, even the most challenging circumstances reveal themselves to be specific forms of the love force in disguise.

The glyph for Venus is a circle atop a cross. This is a symbol for femininity, as well as the symbol for Venus' hand mirror. The glyph represents a valuable truth that the love force is connective, reflecting ourselves to ourselves. All beauty that you find outside of yourself can also be found inside of you. Likewise, when dealing with beauty, we are dealing with something inherently feminine because it attracts and magnetizes energy toward it.

The relationship of the circle and cross in this glyph shows that when Venus energy is properly honored, the superconscious principle of light will rule on the earth plane. That is to say: harmony and love will prevail.

♂ Mars

In the same way the Sun and Moon are envisioned as cosmic lovers, Mars and Venus are star-crossed lovers—lovers who literally cross paths in the sky and have crosses as portions of their glyphs.

Mars and Venus work together to coalesce and move energy as the force of desire. In AstroYoga, Mars energy is considered as the one and only force in the body. This is the force that can manifest as muscular action, emotional expression, sexual expression, and the rising kundalini. Mars is your energy, motivation, drive, and agitation.

In mythology, Mars, or Ares, is the god of war, martial arts, and conflict. He has a sense of bravery about him, and also the protection and assurance that comes from adequate training. Mars is also thought to be related to agriculture, which makes sense when you realize that his purpose is seeking the delight promised by Venus, who often lives in a cultivated, flourishing garden.

In Roman mythology, Mars is the son of Jupiter, which establishes his origin. As such, when the planets are in harmony, Mars is subject to those facets of reality that Jupiter represents, namely the composite Truth of all reality. The Mars principle works best when under the direction of big-picture Truth.

The domiciles of Mars and Venus are always zodiac opposites that complement each other. Think of two ends of a magnet that work together to create a unified magnetic field: this is similar to how Mars and Venus operate in their domicile spectrums. There's a masculine spectrum (Aries-Libra) and a feminine spectrum (Taurus-Scorpio) for these lovers. These spectrums were discussed more fully in chapter three.

Mars is at home in Aries where he directs his energy outward, toward those expressive states that he most wants to embody. He works in Aries to gain greater perspective through the Aries-ruled capacity to think and direct one's thoughts. Mars is also at home in Scorpio, where he takes action either for sexual reasons or for moving the energy of the body into the higher spiritual centers for enlightenment.

As well, Mars is exalted in Capricorn, where his energy is put to use in the slow, steady task of doing gradual work for the joy of work itself, and not for recognition. Capricorn is the sign in which Mars is most likely to reach truly great heights.

The glyph for Mars is a circle with an arrow emerging diagonally upward to the right. This is a symbol for masculinity, as well as a symbol for a shield and spear. This glyph's symbolism suggests that if you want to use the Mars force at a high level, some degree of audacity and bravery is needed. The drive you have to express yourself is best demonstrated through action. Mars is depicted as a war god for this reason: the right use of the Mars force is one where you're dedicated, protected, and able to face challenges through alignment with your personal will, which is a microcosm of the one Will of the universe.

The relationship of the circle and cross in Mars' glyph hints at the right use of this force. Mars is directional, and so it's important to take care in directing the Mars force to a destination where you'd actually like to go.

The glyph shows action that originates from a circle, or superconscious reality. It's important to always begin from a place of wholeness when taking action, to ensure alignment where you're taking steps toward your desire, instead of running away from your fears. That the arrow points upward is an indication you must aim for the highest, though you may also aim toward external desire. Some beings will be called to direct their energy in various ways throughout this life, and it should always be in service of your personal highest ideals as directed by your own inner spark.

♃ Jupiter

Jupiter is the king of the gods, and he goes by many names. In Greek he is Zeus, and he is also known as Jove through Latin derivatives. Zeus and Jove are names which etymologically form roots for deity names such as Jesus (derived from the Latin for 'hail Zeus') and for the words 'yes,' 'joy,' and 'jovial.'

In astrology, Jupiter represents the capital 'T' Truth. He has the distinct ability to expand whatever he touches, which has the useful tendency to help people recognize truth. Consider that when something is small, it may easily be ignored: a small lie, a small mess, a small challenge. But when something expands, you find the truth of what it is, and also a truth of an aspect of who you are. To use the previous examples, a person who habitually lies, a huge disaster of a mess, or a large life challenge will show you a lot more about a person, location, or situation than they will when they're small.

Even though when things are expanded they might not initially feel amazing, Jupiter's expansion is always done for your benefit. As the saying goes: the truth shall set you free. Jupiter shows us all the ways we have deluded ourselves and offers a better approach: the radical acknowledgement of Truth.

In mythology, Jupiter is the father of Pallas-Athena, the goddess of wisdom, and also Mars, the god of war. When you see truth clearly, and are acting in service of Jupiter's traits of jovial energy and joy, then wisdom and right action prevail in your life. Ultimately, this is what allows us to expand into our microcosm of accurately assessed truth that originates within.

Jupiter is at home in Sagittarius. When found in Sagittarius he operates to expand your understanding of the world through higher states of philosophy, broad-reaching travel, and openness to people and ideas beyond your worldview. Jupiter is also at home in Pisces, where he expands the personal rationality to include the logic of the universe.

In the same way that Mars and Venus rule opposite signs, Jupiter rules signs that are opposite to Mercury's zodiac homes. In this way they work together and balance one another. In order to see the Jupiterian capital 'T' Truth, there has to be an expansion of the personal Mercurial mind. If we are attached to old ways of seeing things, true joy eludes us, but when we surrender the subjective mind to Truth, then expansion, joy, and luck are ours.

Jupiter finds his exaltation in Cancer, hinting that Jupiter's highest expression is in the Cancerian-ruled roles of nurture and aligning the psychic centers of the brain with themes of ultimate truth. This will be more fully explained as you read later chapters.

Jupiter's glyph is made of a sideways crescent facing left, and a cross facing right. Hidden in this glyph is the truth that it is the subconscious that elaborates things for us in the manifest plane. One of the subconscious functions is elaboration and growth. For example, when you plant a seed, you may not be aware of its nature, but when the plant grows, you see the truth. This glyph is said to both represent the eagle (Jupiter's bird in mythology) as well as a Z for Zeus (Jupiter's Greek counterpart). These references to Zeus and the eagle refer to an absolute state of freedom that serves as a reminder of the old Jupiterian maxim that the truth shall set you free.

♄ Saturn

Saturn is a secret key to the puzzle of AstroYoga. In the same way that Mars and Venus rule opposite signs, Saturn rules the signs opposite to the domiciles of the Sun and Moon. In AstroYoga, we often become focused on the brightest placements, and give little attention to points of challenge or the mundane habits of life. Yet through these opposing homes of the Sun, Moon, and Saturn, we see that Saturn is a necessary foil and complement to the light.

In mythology, Saturn is a god of harvest and also a god of time. Saturn is the slowest-moving planet that can be seen with the naked eye, and in astrology he represents our path of maturation. A Saturn cycle is roughly 28 years; this path of maturation can be seen most easily in the initial cycle, when we progress from infancy to adulthood. Puberty occurs midway, when Saturn is in the opposite sign of the zodiac.

Saturn represents work, time, and limitations, and because of this, he often receives a bad reputation. While limitations and the steady pace of time can terrify even the bravest people when they consider what it means to be an embodied being, these same limitations also point us toward our most authentic light.

Life is at its best when it takes a definite shape; this tends to be true on all levels of human existence. Since our most basic desires and ideals need a definite form or outlet in order to be realized, Saturn can be used to do the work to form material reality according to our desires and needs. As well, higher forms of spiritual life are at their best when they are integrated into the human body and modes of activity; work and your present perceived limitations have the capacity to be spiritual practice. This is where yoga embodiment practices connect to a chief mystery of astrology. Those who recognize the importance of this connection between the universal and the distinctly embodied will more fully understand the gifts in AstroYoga.

Saturn teaches something important: the path to enlightenment is marked by corresponding changes in the tangible, physical world. This very principle is at play when modern scientists measure changes in the brain and blood chemistry of long-time meditators.

Saturn is at home in Capricorn and Aquarius. These two signs deal with the definite application of time, work, and limitation through both the manifest plane in Capricorn and the mental plane in Aquarius. Saturn finds his exaltation in Libra, a sign connected to the balance of karma and mental drive to equanimity. This hints that the definite Saturnian approach to mental balance can restore equilibrium in the wavering field of karma.

Saturn's glyph is a cross atop a downward-facing crescent. This symbol looks like a sickle, a reference to Saturn's place in harvest. You can also see the allusion to Saturn as the reaper of time walking alongside us as we live our lives. The cross atop the crescent places emphasis on the physical plane, while acknowledging that it's the subconscious plane of life that inevitably supports and sustains the physical.

The Sun, Moon, Mercury, Venus, Mars, Jupiter, and Saturn make up the seven classical planets of Hellenistic and other types of astrology. The seven original planets that are visible to the naked eye are the planets that correspond to the chakra system, the metals of alchemy, and the seven spheres of heaven. A primary focus should be given to these planets when practicing AstroYoga or considering the personal astrology chart.

The Lunar Nodes: Rahu and Ketu

The lunar nodes are Rahu and Ketu, the two-part dragon of Indian astrology and mythology, who direct a stream of energy in the chart. The story of Rahu and Ketu comes from the story of the churning of the ocean of consciousness. In the story, the gods are churning the ocean of consciousness, creating various forms. From the ocean comes the amrita, the divine nectar of immortality and bliss. Only the deities were supposed to drink the amrita, but a demon dragon also had a sip. The gods cut him in half, but had to place his immortal head and tail in the sky as Rahu (the head and north node) and Ketu (the tail and south node).

The lunar nodes Rahu and Ketu aren't physical, but are mathematical points that connect the orbital of the moon with the ecliptic. As such, these are important points in astrology charts that tie the Sun, Moon, and Earth together.

The lunar nodes also dictate when and where eclipses occur in the zodiac. Eclipses can only take place within 18 degrees of a lunar node, with solar eclipses coinciding with new moons and lunar eclipses coinciding with full moons. In astrology, both the lunar nodes and eclipses have a reputation for being foreboding, mainly because at the most basic level people have a tendency to fear change, and change is a guarantee of the lunar nodes.

The lunar nodes show the continuum from karma (action, and the results from past action) to dharma (your soul-aligned path of growth). In the natal chart, this nodal axis shows how a person is capable of growing, changing, and developing in this lifetime. In the transiting chart, these lunar nodes indicate the shifting energetic direction for all of humanity, which changes focus roughly every 18 months.

As an exercise, consider any 18 month period in your life and reflect on whether you experienced a shift in that time, and in what ways. In most cases, fundamental growth takes hold, and these shifts occur on both the societal and personal levels.

The fear of these nodal points comes from the fear we have of change and challenge. However, behind the challenging exterior of these lunar nodes is an invitation. In the natal horoscope, the nodes challenge you to be all you can be, to integrate the opposite, and to take a larger stance in this life. In transit, they encourage you to see your obstacles and enemies as masks hiding the face of love, inviting you into the challenging but benevolent understanding that there is more to you than you realize, and that you can learn to access it.

The glyphs for the lunar nodes are crescents that face each other in the same manner as parentheses. Consider that the direction in which life moves operates largely through the human subconscious. Often we do not know what drives us or what drives society; we only see these energies at play. Remember that subconsciousness can create whatever is impressed upon it.

A note on the lunar nodes: Along with the Sun, Moon, Mercury, Venus, Mars, Jupiter, and Saturn, the lunar nodes make up the Navagrahas in most forms of astrology from India. Navagrahas roughly translates from Sanskrit as the nine holders, nine planets, or nine seizers. The planets are referred to as grahas because they hold or seize everything: all of manifest reality is realized through them. This has a direct correlation to the manner in which the planetary forces operate through the body, and is an excellent topic for deep contemplation.

The lunar nodes are a reminder that you have complete control over your inner world and that your outer world reflects your inner world back to you. This is a great reason to become more conscious of your inner plane through yoga, self-reflection, and meditation. At the same time, the inner world of all humanity creates the outer world of all humanity. We ultimately will succeed together, but the way to create success for others is by creating it for yourself and sharing it.

So, if you've ever longed for an improvement in your life in some way, do not fear the lunar nodes. Instead, befriend them with an attitude of courage in the face of fear, and see what good things your AstroYoga practice and your natal chart have to offer.

⛢ Uranus

Uranus is named for a sky deity. In mythology, he is the father of Saturn and the grandfather of Jupiter. At times, Uranus and Saturn had an inimical relationship, each struggling for power over the other. This translates well to an understanding of exactly what Uranus represents in relationship to Saturn, because Uranus is the planet known for breaking down barriers and creating a sense of freedom and possibility. This is contrary to Saturn's energy, which builds structures and maintains form.

In modern astrology, Uranus occasionally creates a sense of apprehension among chart interpreters. This is because transiting Uranus ushers in change. Uranus is the higher vibration of Mercury, and he operates quickly in order to break apart limiting ideas about how things 'should' be. Uranus often shows us true freedom by disintegrating false structures in a flash. When we have attachment to false images of self, Uranian change can feel like a loss of something precious, rather than a gain in freedom.

However, despite the apprehension some feel toward Uranus, the energy of Uranus is ultimately positive, when approached from a yogic, philosophical perspective. Uranus is a planet of heaven—not the limited cinematic or religious view of heaven, but the concept of what it means to live in a heavenly (harmonious, peaceful, beautiful, loving, content) place in the eternal present moment. Since he is in vibrational alignment with Mercury, it's clear that a heavenly state has a lot to do with the proper alignment of the personal mind.

Uranus is at home in Aquarius and is considered to be the modern ruler of Aquarius. It has been predicted that the Aquarian Age, which is now beginning, is a time when people will succeed in creating a state of heaven on Earth for all embodied beings. The challenges of your present moment serve to spur the right action of creating this harmonious future, which is already now taking form. Uranus shows how to find freedom and harmony in the present, for those who fearlessly embody their true Self in the face of change.

> Uranus, Neptune, and Pluto are the outer planets, which modern exoteric astrology only included after the outer planets' public discoveries in the last few centuries. These planets move in patterns which are considered generational, rather than personal, and can give clear insights into the character of a generation or broad swath of time. Outer planets are higher vibrational emanations of the inner planets, and you can consider them as layers in the harmonic, ever-changing structure of longer periods of time that affect humanity beyond the scope of any single human life.

Furthermore, Aquarius is a sign of innovation and of envisioning and imagining the future as bright. Aquarius is an energy that allows people to take in information that has always been present, but that has been ignored due to ignorance, expectation, or self-fulfilling thinking. Uranus facilitates the open mind and open heart combination signified by this sign.

Uranus' glyph depicts a foundation in superconscious energy, and shows the light of the Sun (circle) as the basis for self-consciousness and subconsciousness. This combination implies the embodied energy and desire of humankind in harmony with the raw energy of the Sun. Heaven, it turns out, is our experience of ourselves in harmony. This is possible now.

♆ Neptune

Neptune is named for the trident-yielding god of the sea. People have always been both enthralled and terrified by the sea, and Neptune's energy reflects this. Neptune promises a dream, but he also might offer you false stops with sirens' songs along your path. Neptune is a transpersonal force, which represents the domain of dreams. Neptune is the modern ruler of Pisces. This corresponds to an association of Neptune with spirituality, the dream state, as well as the fluid nature of reality, hidden by manifest forms. Neptune is also the higher octave of Venus, connecting him with the concept that when forms dissolve, they will ultimately reveal that no matter their original appearance, their true nature is love.

The Neptunian dream realm is one that holds great mystery for human beings, and we access it in myriad ways. We dream when we sleep, astral travel, or journey. We day-dream when we allow our consciousness to wander, and we have aspirational dreams that we hope to realize in waking life. We also experience the unsavory manifestation of dreams: those nightmarish visions during sleep, as well as waking nightmares that arise when mechanisms of escape go wrong and halt the ability to engage with life. A common way Neptunian dreams go awry is through living in a waking dream to avoid reality, whether through fantasy, escape mechanisms, or substances.

Like submerging salt in water, Neptune's effect is that things begin to dissolve in order to align and attune more with the spiritual realms we go to when we dream. In the dream state, collective imagination takes form, and symbols are the primary language of significance. Neptune has the quality of both hiding truth from plain sight, and also revealing truth slowly over time.

Through Neptune's transits, several outcomes are possible. First, the invisible becomes visible. For example, themes hidden in your dreams may reveal your hidden desires. Second, the impossible becomes possible. For example, innovations in humanity begin in the Neptunian imagination before emerging as realities. Third, dream states begin to merge with reality. For example, people achieve their dreams, or on a darker note, coping mechanisms take over life through addiction.

Neptune teaches how to see through what is apparent into what actually is. By dissolving false appearances and by making your dreams true apparitions in the material world, Neptune does his work. If you can learn to sail with Neptune's energy, then the dream we are all living and co-creating in this fluid, changing world is likely to emerge as a living, conscious presence in your life and your AstroYoga practice.

Neptune's glyph appears as a trident, the symbol and scepter of Neptune. It shows the rising of the subconscious water principle over self-consciousness. This is a good time to remind you that the subconscious element is always influenced by self-conscious awareness. When subconsciousness is given free-reign or we become consciously negligent, then all sorts of dreams and nightmares might emerge. Neptune is the planet that will show you what is hidden in your own subconscious, and your other personal planets will show you how to work with what emerges. Neptune reveals much about how to understand the hidden aspects of yourself and of collective humanity.

Pluto

Pluto is named for the Roman form of Hades, the god of the Underworld. In popular culture, he is often depicted as a sort of devil figure, although this is far from the approach that is appropriate in astrology. Pluto constitutes something of a grim reaper, it's true, but there's much more to him than that: he is the shadow and the transformational force.

Consider Pluto as a form of the dark shepherd who rules the shadows where we either cannot look or are afraid to look. The realms hidden from your present consciousness generally include the pre-birth and after death states, as well as certain forms of memory or the akashic record which your conscious mind repressed for one reason or another. Pluto is a higher resonance of Mars, and represents those forces that don't seem within our personal control, but nonetheless are a manifestation of the force of love and action. Pluto is the modern ruler of Scorpio, and represents the transformation that is possible when we channel our Scorpio-ruled life force in particular ways.

Frequently in my work, I've met with pregnant mothers-to-be who have a prominent Pluto transit in their charts surrounding the birth of their child. Typically, this is met with some alarm by the mother, calling to mind the association of Pluto with death. Yet, just as surely as life leaves the physical body at death, life also enters the body at birth, and the same force is at play. This is simply to say, while Pluto's mythology might seem intimidating at first, do not be fooled by appearances: the darkness is truly still only an aspect of the light, and the unknown does not mean the inimical.

Pluto represents transformation. Pluto, as the god of the underworld, represents the transformation of birth to life to death to birth again. These are metaphors for the many transformations we experience in our day-to-day lives. Transformation and transmutation always require facing what is lurking just beneath the level of the conscious mind. To make a better future, the ills of the present must be addressed, and to live a happy life, those energies keeping you in habitual patterns of suffering must also be addressed. Behind Pluto's spooky mask is a divine friend and a source of immense power, if you learn to work with this force.

Abiding in the shadow of Pluto is not ideal, but learning to face what hides in the shadows, especially if it's a piece of yourself, is the only way to step fully into the light. Pluto's glyph depicts subconsciousness lifted above self-consciousness, while receiving input from superconscious solar energy. This glyph depicts a positive application of Pluto, when self-conscious ego awareness is put aside in favor of intuition and connection guided by the light of true conscious awareness.

Not Sure Where To Begin?

It takes time to understand just how important these planetary concepts are. We can be thankful as practitioners to have the representations of planets shown as actors in the play of the cosmic intelligence. The reality is their presence is fractally and harmonically woven throughout the entire universe, so you'll be able to build on the understanding of what these planetary forces bring to your life and your AstroYoga practice.

Can you think about the energies of the planets existing as accessible forces and intelligences that exist both within you and externally to you? If so, you can use their influences to guide your life, work, dreams, and yoga practice to make a better life. You can call upon them with knowledge of what they represent and utilize their influences by activating their placements in your life.

Get to know the planets as you would a group of close friends. You can take them at their surface-level appearance in an instant, but in a lifetime you'll get to know the subtle processes they rule, as well as the energies present within yourself that they are reflecting back to you through your life and your AstroYoga practice.

Take care to spend quality time with the planets that seem favorable to you and that are favorably aspected in your chart, which we'll discuss more later on. As well, spend time with those planets that strike a degree of apprehension in you; they are also a part of you.

Just as you wouldn't expect to fully get to know a person in a day of chatting, realize the more time you spend with the planets, the more they will reveal to you. The wisdom of the planets operates according to the cosmic order, and by studying these forces, you're sure to find many treasures over time in your AstroYoga practice.

Chapter 5: The Zodiac, Planets, and the Physical Body

Key Points in this Chapter
- The zodiac signs contain rich symbolism about the path of life, astrology, and yoga.
- Each zodiac sign relates to particular body parts and processes.
- Practicing yoga in relation to particular bodily areas connects you with specific zodiac signs and planets, and vice versa.

Unlocking the Secrets of the Zodiac in AstroYoga

As you may remember from chapter three, the spectrum of human personality can be charted across the energetic symbolism encoded in the signs of the zodiac. In AstroYoga, the human personality is an emanation of the body, and every human experience happens through the body's physical and energetic capacities. Therefore, the body is the very thing that defines us as human and allows us to experience human life.

No matter how highly you operate in thought or spirit, there will always be a physical correspondence in your body to energetic, mental, or spiritual practice. The connection among the zodiac, body, and spirit is the essence of AstroYoga.

The ways our bodies function and how we experience life correspond to the more widespread astrological influences precipitating through our place in space and time.

Understanding the zodiac is so much more than reconciling a list of functions with a list of zodiac signs; it is a process by which you will understand the character and function of your body and your existence on this plane. If you take nothing else away from this book, the physical correspondence of the zodiac to the body is the conceptual framework to consider.

Every zodiac sign must be in proper balance for each individual's astrology chart and body. As well, care must be taken that the signs are emphasized in a truly positive way. Do your best to use the signs in the highest way you're able in order to create a sense of well-being, health, and harmony in your life.

The Zodiac Signs

♈ Aries

Aries is the ram, or lamb of the sky. You may have heard cultural references to Aries anytime an innocent lamb or lamb's blood is mentioned. In this case, innocence is a reference to Aries being the first sign, and therefore pure as a new cycle begins. The connection of blood to the lamb refers to Mars (the red planet and Aries' ruler) and the equinox sunrise (when the fiery sun enters Aries and returns to the Northern Hemisphere).

The vernal equinox marks the start of Aries season in tropical time and the beginning of a new astrological year. In a new cycle, Aries is the energy that will guide you aright when you know how to harness it. Aries in the zodiac represents the spark of spirit that is alive within each individual and the ability to direct it in particular ways. Connecting with your inner Aries spark is an important first step to any endeavor because the origin point for a well-lived life must stem from the awareness of your inner flame, as well as the courage it takes to act upon your inner drive.

When you act in alignment with your inner flame, things will tend to unfold well. Even though by external appearances challenges may still arise, your inner, clear, Aries-ruled vision will guide you. The inner spark of Aries is something alive in you which is pure, innocent, and unaffected by misguided steps built on false assumptions. This spark directs you toward who and what your soul most wants to explore in this life.

Acting from the Aries flame means acting with integrity, passion, and confidence. It's a necessary first step in any cycle, because it means that wherever your path guides you, your steps will be aligned with the particular purposes of your soul.

Aries in the Body

Aries rules the top of the head, the face, and the eyes. In utero, the face of every human is formed when the heart, which develops atop the brain, slides down toward its place, developing the face as it goes. Your face is literally an expression of your head and your heart, and as the saying goes, your eyes are the window to your soul.

As discussed earlier, Aries implies innocence, and an important truth is found here: every soul is inherently innocent. We all miss the mark in our actions from time to time, but in the spirit of every person is a spark of perfection. This is reflected in yoga philosophy as well as Western schools of esoteric thought. The spirit is a powerful thing, and the visions it creates in the Aries-ruled mind are potent. These mental visions direct the Mars force of the body. Mars is the force that gives tone to muscle and impulse to nerves so we may take our visions from thought-forms to action. This first zodiac sign offers wisdom as well as a warning: your own reasoning, will, and vision must be your guide, in order to safeguard against the passive acquiescence to wills not aligned with yours.

Above all, Aries in the body rules action. When we accept the fact that something in us is pure and innocent, and that innocent spark offers us a vision for our best lives, then it's essential to learn to take action in alignment with your vision. This is why Aries is associated with the martial arts. You must be willing to act upon your vision, and even fight for it. Be particularly willing to battle adversaries you find in your own mind, trying to keep you in a cage of your own design.

Work with Aries energy to hone your vision, clear your head, and create regularity and personality in your expression and face. Notice how you feel physically, and whether you have enough energy to act. Also, take note of any changes in the facial skin or muscle tone.

	Aries At-A-Glance
Tropical Zodiac Solar Transit	March 21-April 19
Modality and Element	Cardinal Fire
Rulership	Mars
Exaltation	Sun
Physical Connections	Head, Face, Eyes
Chakra	Manipura (Solar Plexus)

 Taurus

Taurus is the bull and is considered to be the sign of Mother Earth and the proverbial first woman. One symbol for Earth is a cross (the letter Tau or T). Also, Rus, from Taurus, is a root meaning red or rosy. Putting these together, any time you see a cultural depiction of a rose on a cross or a T, it's a reference to Taurus. This can be helpful for deciphering many popular symbols of the bull and its meaning.

Phonetically, Taurus relates to the word toros and the concepts implied by the toros field. The toros field is the magnetic shape of the Earth and also the shape of the human aura, both connected with astrological ideas of the earth element. The earth element and energetic field of the Earth relate to concepts of Earth mother deities. The Taurus depiction as a bull is likely a reference to Hathor, an Earth mother goddess whose symbol was the cow in Ancient Egypt.

Taurus season marks the sustained energy of the heart of spring, or autumn in the Southern Hemisphere. This time represents an energy of the sustained beauty of the ever-present moment. Taurus represents what we value. This includes those practical resources that we use to sustain our work as well as those inner qualities that we uncompromisingly cherish in ourselves and prize in others.

Taurus energy brings the peace that comes with always having enough in the present moment. This isn't to say that in limited moments we don't experience lack. However, when we align with our Aries-ruled vision, we adopt the perspective of creating and sustaining abundance, no matter what the starting place. It reminds us of the esoteric truth that all that ever was or will be already is, and that we can see it if we use our Aries-ruled vision to find clarity. When we set our vision aright, we begin to experience, enjoy, and delight in the manifest world—this is the essence of Taurus.

Taurus is the first sign in the zodiac ruled by Venus, and as such represents something precious and life-bestowing. Taurus is also the site of the exaltation of the Moon, indicating that the highest expression of subconscious energy is found in the positive expression and embodiment of this sign. Holding Taurus energy in alignment means acting according to your values and creating space for what you love in your life.

Taurus in the Body

Taurus rules the jaw and neck. These are areas of the body that are often not given much thought, since they're not flashy. But, like Taurus, they are essential for living life in a beautiful, healthy way.

Contained within the neck are a number of essential, important bodily functions, many of which are still only partially understood today by even the most schooled experts. Your neck contains neural pathways so complex that they influence every movement of the body, both voluntary and involuntary. Your neck and lower brain control your limbic system and how you enter into parasympathetic (rest and digest) or sympathetic (fight, flight, fawn, or freeze) response. Also, your neck contains essential lymph nodes that are primary in your immune system, your thyroid that controls metabolism, the passageways for both air and food, as well as certain mystical nerve clusters that are essential in working with the higher capacities of the self. Note that these mystical centers in the neck are of primary importance when understanding why the Moon is exalted in Taurus; the subconsciousness is responsible for the physical alignment required for awakening certain nerve centers in the body and brain.

People mention necks the most when they have complaints: tension in the neck, swelling in the lymph nodes, aching in the throat, or issues with thyroid function. Taurus is the first feminine sign of the zodiac, and as such it is the primary sign that reflects physical and mental states in the body. If you'll remember from the lunar discussion, the feminine principles of astrology are what relate to the messaging of the body and the formation of health. When you receive these sorts of messages in the Taurus-ruled sections of the body, they are offering you advice on how to best align yourself with a state of wellbeing.

Work with the Taurus energy to create a sense of harmony with your body and your subconsciousness, as well as to find a sense of relaxation, ease, and abundance in your life.

♉ Taurus At-A-Glance	
Tropical Zodiac Solar Transit	April 20-May 20
Modality and Element	Fixed Earth
Rulership	Venus
Exaltation	Moon
Physical Connections	Jaw, Neck
Chakra	Anahata (Heart)

♊ Gemini

Gemini is the twins. You may have heard cultural references to Gemini in stories and mythos about twins, especially those where the twins are in opposition to one another. Gemini is Castor and Pollux (cleanliness and pollution) in the Greco-Roman tradition, Cain and Abel in Judaeo-Christianity, and other sets of fraternal opposites.

Gemini energy in the zodiac represents that liminal time when spring begins to turn to summer, or autumn to winter in the Southern Hemisphere. Gemini energy brings the quickening, circulating quality of air that is common in many climates during Gemini season.

When Gemini energy is harnessed, things tend to move quickly and energies tend to be spent on play, communication, and exploring the local environment.

From the mythologies of Aries to Gemini comes an important truth. While Aries initiates the cycle with innocence and the spark of life, and Taurus responds to Aries as our subconscious working in our favor, Gemini implies that we are given a choice in how to proceed. Namely, it's possible to progress in such a way that the outcomes are either favorable or unfavorable. This is a significant point: there's no bypassing the manifest world in yoga or astrology, and occasionally human beings embody both twins in this sign.

Gemini is an air sign ruled by Mercury, the planet of the mind. Here is an important clue to this sign: the mind is both something you can change and also something you can use to create change. As well, in every situation in the manifest world, you have the distinct option of taking a different vantage in order to shift your conclusion toward a more positive end. In Gemini you have the capacity to change and choose a better path.

Gemini in the Body

Gemini rules the lungs, shoulders, arms, hands, and nervous system. Hands are one of the primary symbols for human kind. In fact, the word man shares a linguistic root for the words for hands and mind. Manas in Sanskrit means mind. In the Indo-European language family this root moves to words such as manus, which is Latin for hand. Furthermore, we often notice people who speak with their hands or who drum their fingers in order to speak. Additionally, the only human language not predominantly carried out via voice is sign language, which fully utilizes the hands and arms. The hands, arms, shoulders, and nervous system are obvious in their utility, but also fairly finicky. The shoulder joint is the most mobile joint in the body, but also one of the easiest to dislocate. Likewise, the wrists have great intricacy and are capable of weight-bearing in a number of positions, but are also liable to experience nerve issues. As well, the nervous system is an obvious boon to the human being, but it can easily be thrown off its course through stress and nerve disorders.

The Gemini-ruled lungs are one of two places in the body where prana is taken in; the other is the colon. Remember that Gemini always offers you a choice, and the first choice you have in any situation is to breathe well or poorly. Your breath, in turn, affects the Gemini-ruled nervous system, which influences all areas of life. This is a central concept related to Gemini energy: your small choices are responsible for carving your path and your wellbeing in a world of myriad possibilities.

Physically, you may consider the movement of Gemini like a spiral. You can either spiral away from wellbeing or spiral toward higher and higher forms of health. Your mind and habitual thought patterns, as well as what you do, determine where your spiral is heading. In modern yoga asana classes, two of the most common injuries occur at the shoulder and wrist. Most often, these are repetitive use injuries, which occur from misalignment in practice, habitually repeated. At the same time, many modern yoga asana practitioners can have some of the stronger wrists and shoulders in the human form, due to the habitual right motion through these areas.

Gemini reminds us that we have a choice, if we just think about it. Take care to examine what you're doing in your form as well as what you're accepting as truth in your mind. Ask yourself often whether the opposite of your thoughts might also be a true conclusion.

Work with Gemini energy to create a sense of personal choice and vantage in your body and mind, a healthy expression of your mind through what you do with your hands, and an embodied clarity in your nervous system and breath.

Chapter 5: The Zodiac, Planets, and the Physical Body

⚏	Gemini At-A-Glance
Tropical Zodiac Solar Transit	May 21–June 20
Modality and Element	Mutable Air
Rulership	Mercury
Physical Connections	Lungs, Shoulders, Arms, Hands, Nervous System
Chakra	Vishuddha (Throat)

♋ Cancer

Cancer is the crab, and the predominant symbol of home and motherhood in the zodiac. While Taurus represents Mother Earth energy, Cancer represents the ways in which each of us nurture, care for, and protect what we hold most dear. Cancer is the first water symbol of the zodiac, and more than any other sign, it's connected with the sea and the Moon. The feminine, the sea, and the Moon have been connected throughout history due to their physical similarities and symbolic implications. Both the sea and the Moon move through cycles of ebb and flow, waxing and waning. Additionally, the watery sea and the Moon imply reflection, with the Moon reflecting the polarized light of the Sun and the surface of water serving as a natural mirror. They both also symbolize nurture, home, and rest, since the sea feeds us and is the origin of many life forms, and the Moon rules the night, when people return home to renew their bodies in sleep.

> I'm often asked about the naming of the series of physical ailments known as cancers in medicine, and their association, if any, with the zodiac sign Cancer. The answer in brief is that the disease was originally named by the Greek physician Hypocrites to describe tumors, which often appeared crab-like in nature. Most physicians at the time would have studied medical astrology, so it's likely that Hypocrites was also aware that the zodiac sign Cancer connects to ideas of multiplication, which is one unfortunate tenet of the disease. Having significant placements in Cancer (or any sign for that matter) does not directly imply the occurrence of this or any disease.
>
> In astrology, disease in the body is only read retroactively. This is because all placements may be reconciled for a place of health, and so no placement preemptively implies disease. Medical astrology is used as a diagnostic tool only after disease has arisen in a person. Until that point, medical astrology is used as a way of optimizing health, which is largely where AstroYoga practices come into play.

Cancer initiates at the summer solstice in the North when the Sun is at his zenith, indicating an element of fire (life and spirit) being present in her waters. Fire in water is something you may often come across in the study of AstroYoga, and it represents the spark of spirit which is present in manifest life forms. Through all the qualities mentioned so far, Cancer reminds us who and what we are. Quite literally, we are mainly water, occupied with a certain cohesion of spirit. Cancer in the zodiac reminds us to come home to ourselves in moments of reflection and self-nurture.

The symbolism of the crab reminds us of two things. The first is that we can be at home wherever we go, just like the crab who carries her home on her back. The second is that we each have pieces of ourselves that are soft and need nurturing, and if those areas are neglected or hurt, we each have a set of metaphoric pincher claws for protection. Use these wisely.

Cancer is ruled by the Moon, and Jupiter is exalted in Cancer. The Moon rules the subconscious, and Jupiter is the planet of universal truth. When the subconscious aspects of life are under the authority of universal truth rather than deception or personal whim, wellbeing and harmonious conditions naturally unfold in life.

Cancer in the Body

Cancer rules the breasts, chest, and stomach. This is an obvious reference to the motherhood connection with Cancer, as babies nurse from the breasts. Additionally, Cancer is associated with nurture and nourishment, which we receive through our stomachs. As well, symbolically when we give selflessly, we say we are 'giving from the heart,' implying the offering through the chest of our most selfless gifts. In the next chapter, you'll see that the front body is the space of energetic outpouring, which is in alignment with the giving aspect of Cancer.

The breasts, chest, and stomach house the waters of the body, holding space for the etherial water of emotion and intuition in the chest, as well as holding the literal waters of digestion in the belly. Here too, we see the combination of fire and water as symbolized by the summer solstice, this time in the acidic, fiery water present as the digestive stomach acid.

The chest serves as our physical home for the true center of the human being, the heart. Similar to the crab with its soft center and bony shell, the Cancerian chest is the watery and bony ribcage which houses the fiery heart.

More than anything, Cancer implies the home and the mother. These are both entities outside the self, yet related to the self; Cancer energy teaches that the physical body is not all there is to us. Like the chariot metaphor seen both in the tarot card associated with Cancer and the Bhagavad Gita, we see that the vehicle for the Self is not the Self. Cancer teaches us that the body and the universe are our homes, but that our true form of spirit abides within and around us.

Work with Cancer energy to create a sense of care, nurture, sustenance, and safety wherever you go. Also use this energy to find and embody the truth that as long as you come home to yourself again and again, victory in all your true endeavors is an inevitability.

Cancer At-A-Glance	
Tropical Zodiac Solar Transit	June 21-July 22
Modality and Element	Cardinal Water
Rulership	Moon
Exaltation	Jupiter
Physical Connections	Breasts, Chest, Stomach
Chakra	Ajna (3rd Eye)

♌ Leo

Leo is the lion, and the ruler of the jungle. As the second fire sign in the zodiac, Leo harmonizes with what Aries represents. Aries sets a plan in motion using reason and foresight; Leo sustains the spirit of personal sovereignty over the personal life force.

A clue as to the important relationship between Leo and Aries comes in their association with the Sun. Leo is ruled by the Sun, and the Sun is exalted in Aries. More connections among Leo, Aries, and the Sun will be made clear in the next chapter when we discuss subtle body associations with the signs.

Leo is the energy of holding your personal light, allowing it to shine. The true personal light comes from within, and if you trace the chemistry and physics back far enough, you'll discover what AstroYoga has always taught: your personal light is composed of the same material as radiant sunlight, simply in a different form. For example, all materials are said to have been forged in the center of stars, and therefore all of manifest reality is composed of ancient stardust. As well, all food comes to us by way of photosynthesis, if it's plant material, and even animal products contain previously consumed plants and are embodiments of the radiant energy of the Sun.

This very light that is associated with Leo is what makes you the sovereign of your domain. To be sovereign means to reign or rule, and it also indicates a high degree of mastery. Interestingly, an antiquated use of the word refers to a measure of gold, the metal associated with the Sun. While modern living might try to trick you into thinking that someone else rules your form, thoughts, or actions, working with the zodiac will show you otherwise, that you always have access to personal rulership, which is freely given and influenced by the light within.

The Sun is primary in astrology, and because of this, no planet is exalted in Leo, since no planet may be exalted above the Sun.

Leo in the Body

Leo rules the heart, upper back, and spine. This is another clue to the relationship among the fire signs thus far in the zodiac: where Aries rules the reasoning portions of the brain as well as the eyesight, Leo rules the center of your being.

In Leo's association with the heart, an important point is made: the heart, not the head, is the true ruler of our personal kingdoms. Yet, as indicated by the harmonious relationship among all fire signs, the head and heart work in harmony with one another.

The role of the Leo-ruled areas of the body is still only partially understood by modern science. The cardiac ganglia connected with Leo is known to connect with pacemaker cells, as well as the sympathetic and parasympathetic nervous systems. In modern science, untangling and fully understanding this network of neurons is still in its early stages. Yet you don't need to dissect every neuron in your body to know that the heart is a space of true wisdom, and like the popular adage that you must 'follow your heart,' it is indeed the ideal ruler of your life. If you're ever lost and need to tap into the true guidance that won't lead you astray, spend a few minutes listening to the beating sound of your own heart. This is the location from which the 'still, small voice' often spoken about will arise and offer you clear direction. Listen for clarity rather than soothsaying or coddling, and you'll find your answer.

Work with Leo energy to create a sense of personal creative sovereignty over your own life. When you're in touch with this energy, you'll find yourself to be a creator of a life infused with the special light that you hold within.

♌	Leo At-A-Glance
Tropical Zodiac Solar Transit	July 23-August 22
Modality and Element	Fixed Fire
Rulership	Sun
Physical Connections	Heart, Upper Back, Spine
Chakra	Ajna (3rd Eye)

♍ Virgo

Virgo is the virgin, who is usually depicted holding wheat. She is known by many names including the house of bread, since she's related to the harvest, as well as names for virginal goddesses depicted in mythologies and religions. In the same way we see a connection between Taurus and Cancer, we see this theme continued in Virgo. If Taurus connects to the first woman and to Mother Earth, and Cancer to the Moon and all mothers, then Virgo relates to the young woman and the form of the goddess within us, which, though untouched, can produce profound nourishment.

Virgo represents the manner in which we sort things out using deductive mental reasoning in collaboration with inductive mental reasoning. Deductive reasoning implies reasoning elaborated from a premise, rather than reasoning that's tested against all possible premises. Because of this, the energy of Virgo is capable of profound sorting and elaboration, if the original premise is true. If the original premise is false, Virgo is capable of elaborating reasoning in support of a false conclusion.

Therefore, it is important to guard your mind when dealing with Virgo energy and to truly see how the wheat separates from the chaff. When you base your mind in truth and purity, true insights will follow that will be much more profound than insights made from mere inductive reasoning alone. Reasoning based in truth from both arenas is bound to agree once the subtle senses have been fully developed.

Mercury is both at home and exalted in Virgo. One reason for this is that Virgo energy, when rightly used, produces true reasoning that concentrates the Mercury force. Concentration implies a strengthening of the powers associated with Mercury and the mind.

The Riddle of Virgin Birth

Throughout history, mythology and religion have shared stories of enlightened beings born of a virginal goddess or woman. Most relevant to AstroYoga is perhaps the birth of Krishna, the god Vishnu in human form, who is said to be born of the virginal Devaki. As well, though many stories of Buddha exist, in one legend he is born of a virgin named Maya or Mary. Christianity has a virginal birth of the Christ, and Egypt has the virginal birth of the solar god Ra. The list goes on.

Like all symbols, multiple layers of explanation apply to this riddle of virgin birth. Here are two.

On the winter solstice, the Sun stands still. When the Sun appears to move again, the Sun rises in the sky in the sign of Capricorn. The sign Virgo is at the midheaven, ruling over the metaphoric birth of the Sun. Note that deities associated with virgin birth are solar 'sons' in some form.

The solar aspect of these deities is meant to awaken the Soma, Amrita, or Christ, which are all words for the divine nectar. This is the nectar of enlightenment understood to occur when the solar force is raised to the third-eye space. The wise of these traditions tell us that what physically facilitates this process begins in the intestine, which is ruled by Virgo. Therefore, the realization of the solar aspect of yourself begins in the Virgo region of you: the inner deity is born of your personal virgin.

Please note that you'll see references to this topic throughout cultures. The sphinx, with the head of a woman and body of the lion, is one such reference, as well as the modern 'Christmas story' located in Bethlehem, which translates to the house of bread, another name for Virgo.

Virgo in the Body

Virgo rules the intestine. You might have heard the intestine called the 'second brain,' and this association is in agreement with AstroYoga, as Mercury is both at home and exalted in Virgo.

Mercury's exaltation in Virgo implies that something of the force of concentration and the collection of mental power serves its highest purpose in the intestine. At first glance, this might seem silly, but a deeper look will explain one of the primary open secrets in astrology and yoga.

The secret is hidden in plain sight and is this: for every spiritual and mental step toward enlightenment, there is a shift on the physical plane of embodiment

With prolonged yoga and meditation practice, the intestine begins to shift the manner in which it absorbs nutrients from chyme. This alters the blood makeup, which travels to the brain and produces shifts there. This is the physical embodiment of a spiritual phenomenon where more light is made available at the Mercurial self-conscious level of personal perception.

This intestinal connection to higher states of consciousness is why, in so many myths, the enlightened figure comes from a reputed virgin birth. At the external level of interpretation, people wonder at this puzzle or write it off as religious fantastical thinking. But when viewed through this lens, we find a profound truth that the Virgo sections of the body do, in fact, birth the enlightened being. It just so happens that both figures are aspects of you.

Work with Virgo energy to test your assumptions against universal truths. Use Virgo energy to help you organize your life and yourself so that what is within your control may be tended to with insight and consistency.

♍	Virgo At-A-Glance
Tropical Zodiac Solar Transit	August 23–September 22
Modality and Element	Mutable Earth
Rulership	Mercury
Exaltation	Mercury
Physical Connection	Intestine
Chakra	Vishuddha (Throat)

♎ Libra

Libra is the scale of justice, universal law, and karmic balance. Karma is a word often used carelessly in modern culture, so take time to ensure that your understanding of karma is an accurate one.

Karma is a word best translated as action. Actions produce reactions, and this concept of reaction is also included in the concept of karma. Karma can be modified. The Newtonian law is that every action has an equal and opposite reaction. While the Newtonian law is accurate and easily predictable in a controlled environment, in collective reality, actions and reactions are perpetually occurring, so reactions might not always seem predictable if you have failed to see every originating action. Karma is an adherence to universal law. What karma is not, is a form of luck, punishment, reward, or a universal boogyman exacting revenge. You can both create new karma and modify existing karma by taking the right mental measure of a situation.

Libra is an air sign, related to action as directed by the mind. Libra is ruled by Venus, demonstrating that action and reaction are best taken as forms of love and connectivity. Most actions are steps toward unification. When Libra energy is used foolishly, steps are taken away from unification in an ill-imagined attempt to inspire others to love.

A traditional Libra balance is wobbly and easily shifts. Likewise, though individuals often envision their actions producing exact and predictable results, personal karmic action connects with the ever-shifting collective body of action. This shifts easily as all humans are acting and reacting at the same time, constantly modifying and shifting the state of the universal karmic scale.

Saturn is exalted in Libra, and this hints at how the scale of karma can best be balanced. Saturn represents the material world, boundaries, time, diligent work, and the inner structure of matter. Therefore, creating a definite structure and putting in the time and work it takes to shift circumstances for yourself and others is the highest potential for Libra. Like all interpretations of the zodiac, this has implications beyond the personal: the karma of humanity is impacting each of us, and each of us is a personal unit who may, in turn, shift karma for the collective.

Libra in the Body

Libra rules the kidneys, adrenals, skin, lumbar region, endocrine system, and upper buttocks. These regions all embody the responsive nature of karma as related to some of the other signs directly interacting with Libra in the zodiac. The kidneys and adrenals balance our body chemistry, and the low back and skin alert us to imbalances in our bodies. Kidneys serve the purpose of keeping the blood chemistry in the right balance. This is Libra's response to both its harmonious relationship to Aquarius, which rules the blood, and the preceding sign of Virgo, which contributes nutrients that shift the blood chemistry.

The adrenal glands sit atop the kidneys and are an important part of the endocrine system. These glands regulate aspects of metabolism, blood pressure, the immune system, and the stress response. The adrenals are highly responsive to the thoughts and actions inspired by Libra's opposite sign of Aries. Your adrenals are essential to survival, and operate best when unnecessary stress is avoided. Healthy adrenal function stems from healthy actions and proper reasoning from the right use of Aries energy.

Likewise, the skin and low back are areas which experience a healthy response to the proper structuring of life, indicated by Saturn. The low back is often the first place to feel pain when posture is overlooked, and the skin both acts as an environmental boundary and as a screen to see what is happening on the inner plane of the body.

Allow these areas to tell you what action you need to take to modify the outcomes in both your physiology and your experience of life itself. Use Libra energy to determine the balance and boundaries of life in response to action, as well as to modify situations that you'd like to change.

♎ Libra At-A-Glance	
Tropical Zodiac Solar Transit	September 23-October 22
Modality and Element	Cardinal Air
Rulership	Libra
Exaltation	Saturn
Physical Connections	Kidneys, Adrenals, Skin, Lumbar Region, Endocrine System, Upper Buttocks
Chakra	Anahata (Heart)

♏ Scorpio

Scorpio is the scorpion, and also the snake and the eagle. Scorpio is distinct among the signs in that it has three animals associated with it. One reason for this is Scorpio is the fixed sign of water.

A distinct feature of the cosmic water is that it takes on various forms based on the human capacity to imagine, envision, and create. Where the fiery spark in Leo initiates creativity, it's the waters held by Scorpio that get the job done. Scorpio knows that for things to come to fruition in life, the right seed must be planted in the right season and right soil. Consequently, the fruition of what Scorpio represents is a quality associated with Taurus, Scorpio's opposite sign.

The scorpion, snake, and eagle all represent distinct manifestations of the watery potential represented by Scorpio. If left unexamined, potential energy contains both hope and fear because potentiality has the capacity to manifest in several directions. The scorpion depicts a lower manifestation, one concerned with earthly matters, direct application of power, and self-protection. The snake represents the vibratory manifestation of Scorpio energy as the agent of movement and change in this life. And the eagle represents the capacity to use potential power to rise to a greater height and more enlightened viewpoint.

Scorpio is ruled by Pluto in the modern application of planets and traditionally has been ruled by Mars. You may recall that in mythology Mars is associated with war, and Pluto is associated with death. For the purposes of daily life, these planets translate to the Martian force of action and the Plutonian force of change and regeneration. Both action and change imply the perpetual cycle of birth, death, and rebirth on a cellular level. Every action you take in thought or physical motion involves itself in a dance of cellular regeneration, tearing down, death, and rebirth. This cycle of regeneration may seem obvious, but it has deep wisdom hidden in a simple truth: self-directed energy can be what you make it. You are not the static form appearances would have you believe, and when you tap into your inner power, you can transform your energy to make your life what you will.

Scorpio in the Body

Scorpio rules the sexual organs of the body. These glands and organs contain the seed potential for human life and regeneration both on a biological and an energetic level. To understand the manifestation of this seed potency is to understand the three-part connection of Scorpio to the scorpion, snake, and eagle.

Most people are familiar with the physical manifestations of Scorpio connected with the scorpion. These include the physical act of sex, as well as those acts that are not sexual in nature but are conceived and carried out in darkness.

To understand the eagle and snake's connection to the human body requires the knowledge that in AstroYoga there is only one energy that powers the human body. This single energy manifests in disparate forms. In other words, the same potential power the human body has to co-create a child, is the same potential power you use to fuel your body, use your mind, or do anything at all. All forms of human activity, including thought, have a physiological component.

Obviously, all forms of human activity aren't carried out in overt, observable physical action. Some things are accomplished in the vibratory action tied to imagination. Far from make-believe, this form of imagination is tied to the predominating experience you have of yourself and the beliefs that form within you. This vibratory imaginative energy at the personal level is the snake, which is directly tied to the Kundalini/snake goddess potency in yoga.

As you may have heard, the Kundalini force is coiled in the Scorpio region at the base of the spine, and may rise through the chakras when awakened. This is the predominant association with the snake in Scorpio. Kundalini awakenings happen spontaneously and are often temporal, short-lived experiences, albeit ones that make a lasting impression. The third animal connected with Scorpio is the eagle. The eagle represents the expression of Scorpio energy when it remains in an expansive state of heightened awareness. The eagle further represents the personal experience of knowing your own power, and seeing yourself from the highest vantage.

Use Scorpio energy to connect to your personal power and to realize your greatest desires in this life, using the knowledge that everything vibrates and everything is in a constant cycle of change and regeneration.

Chapter 5: The Zodiac, Planets, and the Physical Body

♏	Scorpio At-A-Glance
Tropical Zodiac Solar Transit	October 23-November 21
Modality and Element	Fixed Water
Rulership	Pluto (Modern) Mars (Traditional)
Physical Connection	Sexual Organs
Chakra	Manipura (Solar Plexus)

♐ Sagittarius

Sagittarius is the centaur, with the torso of a human and body of a horse. Sagittarius is the energy that holds the knowledge and wisdom of the stars while living in harmony with nature. In mythology, centaurs tend to be fierce, unruly creatures, but the Sagittarius constellation references Chiron, a centaur known for his gentleness and wisdom. Chiron was a wise teacher who taught many famous students, including Jason and Achilles, about medicine, the arts, and the path of knowledge. Chiron was known for wisdom, which implies knowledge connected with universal truth. This wisdom is precisely what Sagittarius energy represents. In Sagittarius' opposite sign of Gemini, knowledge is known through association. This Gemini knowledge seeks understanding, but is limited by knowledge known locally. Sagittarius builds on Gemini energy by seeking ultimate, universal truths. These are truths that can only be known, never told, since the purity of absolute truth exists beyond linguistic semiotic articulation. In other words, the full truth cannot be limited by language and words, since the full truth includes every reality on every plane.

Because of this, Sagittarius is associated with those pursuits that begin to point us along the path of wisdom. The higher fields of study in education, philosophy, and religion/spirituality, as well as far-reaching travels, all put us into contact with ideas that complicate our original understanding of life as symbolized by Gemini. Sagittarius is a fire sign, indicating that high forms of truth are connected with the fire of spirit and sight, rather than thought.

In mythology, Chiron is immortalized in the constellation Sagittarius by the god Zeus, also known as Jupiter. You may recall that Jupiter is the planet associated with the highest forms of truth, as well as with calling out those ways in which we've deceived ourselves. Jupiter is the ruler of Sagittarius, as all exploration is ultimately a quest for the Truth which has always been present, hiding in plain sight.

Sagittarius in the Body

Sagittarius rules the liver, hips, thighs, and lower buttocks. The most obvious association with what Sagittarius represents is that the hips and thighs are what allow you to walk and travel great distances. The thighs and buttocks contain the largest muscles in the human body. Using these muscles engages the fire element in circulating motion, which is associated with Sagittarius, as it is the mutable fire sign.

Perhaps even more significant than these muscular associations, is Sagittarius' association with the liver. The liver is one of the primary organs needed for life, and also the only organ known to be capable of self-regeneration. Invariably, the health of the liver determines the overall health of the body. In some ancient cultures, the liver was considered as the seat of the soul, used much the same way as modern linguistics uses the heart or the brain (ruled by the other two fire signs). Today, many holistic practitioners recognize the liver's importance in processing emotions such as anger, in addition to the physical role the liver plays in processing food, fat, and trapping toxins. The ultimate truth is what Sagittarius energy seeks, and the truth shall always set you free. In an esoteric sense of the word, freedom indicates freedom from all limitations you now perceive. These limitations can include illness, unease (dis-ease) in the body, limiting belief systems, and the very challenges you look at with an attitude of impossibility. In a parallel manner, the liver represents our capacity to set ourselves free on the physical plane of existence. Listening to your liver and feeding it good things can have beneficial effects in your yoga and meditation practice.

Use Sagittarius energy to connect to truth and dismantle limiting belief systems. Use it also to align your mind with truth so your subconscious builds your body and your practice into a harmonious state.

Sagittarius At-A-Glance	
Tropical Zodiac Solar Transit	November 22-December 21
Modality and Element	Mutable Fire
Rulership	Jupiter
Physical Connections	Liver, Hips, Thighs, Lower Buttocks
Chakra	Svadhisthana (Sacral)

♑ Capricorn

Capricorn is the goat, and also the sea goat, depicted as a goat with a fish tail. In one version of the Capricorn legend, the horned goats are able to traverse the sea until one by one they climb upon land toward the highest peaks. Yet in doing so, they lose their fish tails and therefore their ability to swim.

Even in this brief description of the myth, there are several concepts to be gleaned about Capricorn energy. The first is that Capricorn holds the energy necessary to navigate the watery depths corresponding to emotion, memory, and the fluid nature of all material and potential energy in the universe. The second is that the capacity to navigate the waters can be lost or remembered. The third is that the goat is capable of climbing to great heights, which means navigating the real dangers that exist in climbing to the sharp, rocky peaks.

Capricorn energy represents the capacity to direct both manifest forms and potential energy through steady, consistent steps taken over time. Your steady, daily work rarely receives celebration either from others or yourself. Even so, it often represents a relentless tenacity toward a lofty or deep goal to which you've dedicated yourself, perhaps so long ago that you've forgotten, yet the dedication remains.

Capricorn is ruled by Saturn, the ruler of structure and boundaries within time and space. Saturn grants structure to plans. Capricorn's opposite sign of Cancer is the home of the Moon. Therefore, Capricorn forms the structural basis within which the lunar aspects of life may be expressed. As well, Mars is exalted in Capricorn. Mars rules action and fighting the good fight. This means Mars has his highest expression when practically moving toward long-term goals with vigor and consistency. Mars must be channeled into the specific in order to be his most effective.

Capricorn in the Body

Capricorn rules the knees, joints, and skeletal system. These structural aspects of the physical body have an obvious association with Saturn, the planet ruling definite form and structure. The bones and joints are what give the body physical structure, as well as hold the body's shape in space, even when the muscular system completely relaxes.

The fluid fishtail of Capricorn can be seen in the bones and joints as well. A primary fluid of the body is blood, and blood cells are formed in bone marrow, the spongy material at the center of bones. You may remember that the earth element is always a combination of the other three primary elements. Here we see an interesting relationship of earthy Capricorn as a mixture of fire, air, and water. Most of the body's blood is made in the pelvic, breast, and spinal bones, which are associated with other elements in the body. In the section on Aquarius, you'll see the blood is ruled by Aquarius, an air sign. We've already covered how the spine is associated with Leo's fire and that the breast and pelvic areas are associated with water signs.

Bone health, while often overlooked until such time as a problem arises, is essential for wellbeing. To have healthy bones means to have healthy blood and a good immune system. To have healthy bones also means to have structure, protection, and physical boundaries for the body. Like Capricorn, the ultimate purpose of these physical structures is to be so steady and consistent that they can be relied upon without a second thought.

Use Capricorn energy to steadily drive you toward your loftiest goals, while keeping you in tune with the true nature of the fluid structure of the universe. With steady steps, any goal is attainable.

♑	Capricorn At-A-Glance
Tropical Zodiac Solar Transit	December 22–January 19
Modality and Element	Cardinal Earth
Rulership	Saturn
Exaltation	Mars
Physical Connections	Knees, Joints, Skeletal System
Chakra	Muladhara (Root)

Aquarius

Aquarius is the water-bearer, usually depicted as a young man carrying a vessel of water. Water is the most central consideration when building societies; this is related to the Aquarian association with community and humanitarianism. This also connects to the Aquarian characteristic of innovation, since some of the earliest innovations in civilization had to do with water distribution, bathing, and sanitization.

As well, Aquarius is connected with the right application of the mind. Aquarius is an air sign, but relates closely to the element of water, which refers to the fluid aspect of subconsciousness and manifest reality. Therefore, Aquarian energy connects with the concept that the world of form is responsive to the mind. With Aquarius, we see that when the mind is still, the fluid nature of matter reveals itself, and the mind is able to influence reality in a conscious way.

Perhaps this is one reason why, at the dawning of the Aquarian Age, it has become fashionable to consider how thoughts form reality. Although this popular conception of thoughts forming reality is often articulated in a piecemeal way, it resonates with many because it contains a seed of truth: to a still mind, all of reality is fluid.

The modern ruler of Aquarius is Uranus, and the traditional ruler is Saturn. Those who study the related system of tarot will see something distinct here, as Uranus relates to the first major card and Saturn to the last. Likewise, in mythology, Saturn and Uranus are related: Uranus the father, and Saturn the son. While related, they are contrary to one another. Saturn and Uranus have an inimical familial relationship that contains stories of intense battles. Uranus is the lord of the sky who is expansive and opens life to the experience of total freedom, the svatantra spoken about in yoga. Saturn is the ruler of limitation, who offers material form and boundaries of time and space to the manifest world in order for specificity to exist.

In Aquarius, Uranus and Saturn are both at home, revealing an important truth: the state of absolute, mystic freedom is experienced in specific form. In other words, the perfect state that so many seek to find is already and always available here and now, inside you, as yourself. This, perhaps more than anything else, is the hallmark of Aquarian energy.

Aquarius in the Body

Aquarius rules the ankles, blood, and circulation. Here you can see the Aquarian connection to Saturnian structure in the ankles and Uranian freedom in the circulation. Physically, Aquarian energy manifests as an understanding of where we stand, knowing that our ankles give us the structure that holds us up, and knowing as well that what we stand upon is actually fluid in nature, as will be seen in the section on Pisces in the body. Aquarius associates with the ankles to show that the firm foundation upon which we rest our lives, our ideas, and our societies, is actually considered firm because of its fluidity, rather than in spite of it.

The fluid blood relates to this concept, this time in reference to the fiery aspects of the Leo-ruled heart. Leo is the opposite sign to Aquarius. The Leo message of sovereign, soul-level understanding pumps the Aquarian blood and carries the message of the heart with it. In the relationship between the heart and the blood we see the embodiment of 'may all beings everywhere be happy and free,' translated from the Sanskrit lokah samastah sukhino bhavantu.

The blood contains life force. We know this intuitively as well as societally, since people often gather their Aquarian spirit to donate blood when there are others in need. To understand and embody Aquarian energy more fully will be one of the privileges of this coming age. Try to see beyond the solid appearances of matter, and instead find stillness in your mind and in the steadiness of your own fluidity.

Use Aquarian energy to connect with your life force for the good of all beings, and to find the foundation upon which you stand in your daily life through every season.

Aquarius At-A-Glance	
Tropical Zodiac Solar Transit	January 20-February 18
Modality and Element	Fixed Air
Rulership	Uranus (Modern) Saturn (Traditional)
Physical Connections	Ankles, Blood, Circulation
Chakra	Muladhara (Root)

♓ Pisces

Pisces is the fish, depicting an understanding of the fluid nature of the universe. Unlike the other water signs, Pisces is without defense. Cancer has its pinchers and Scorpio has pinchers and a stinging tail. Both Cancer and Scorpio are depicted by animals that scuttle along the ground, while Pisces has the ability to swim, fully immersed in the etheric water.

Water in the zodiac connects to the fluid nature of the universe, and also to emotion and the shifting nature of the changeable aspects of the mind. As well, water is the primary etheric material connected to the realm of subconsciousness.

This immersion in water is one reason Pisces is associated with qualities of dissolution and the opening of the mind into the fluid, mystic states of being. Pisces energy is related to the arts and mystical states as received intuitively. This concept is echoed within many great discoveries and works of art, with composers and scientists alike saying that their greatest accomplishments simply came to them. And often, these intuitively-accessed revelations arrived while connected in some way to water or fluid activities, such as while bathing.

Pisces is ruled by Neptune, and Jupiter is its traditional ruler. Neptune is connected with the ability to dissolve into the etheric waters, and Jupiter is connected to the ability to expand into truth. Physically, dissolution relates to expansion since when anything dissolves, it expands throughout the watery solution. In this relationship you can see how Neptune and Jupiter connect to the Piscean ability to dissolve solid concepts in order to expand into realms of higher truth.

As the mutable water sign, Pisces represents how the etheric water circulates. Inspiration is available to us all, if we learn to swim in these waters. The secret of Pisces is that the etheric water is present in all things. Even solid forms are fluid when examined beyond the level of appearance, as atoms are formed by constantly moving subatomic forms, which only give the appearance of steadiness. Likewise, time aids this illusion because in a given moment a solid structure exists, yet thousands of years later this structure has dissolved to dust.

Venus is exalted in Pisces, meaning that she has her highest expression in this sign. Here we see that love is seen in her most potent form when she is dissolved and her true nature is revealed. In dissolution, we find Venus permeates all things. This is a mystical truth that opens the doors to higher understanding in the zodiac.

Pisces in the Body

Pisces rules the feet and lymphatic system. The feet are your connection to the earth. They're also sensitive and have connective energetic meridians to the major organs and centers of the body. Additionally, the lymphatic system's primary purpose is moving and balancing the lymphatic waters through the body. These processes help nourish you and protect your body from pathogens. The Piscean lymphatic water is the very mechanism of dissolution in the body; this water dissolves and flushes toxins and also dissolves fats and vitamins in food to be used as nourishment.

The Pisces connection to channeling inspiration relates to Pisces' connection to the feet. The feet are some of the more sensitive areas of the body, where physical meridians terminate to connect with anything the feet touch. This connection is a channel for energy to enter and leave the body. Essential oil foot massage, reflexology, and grounding are all practices centered upon the feet as energetic doorways.

The Pisces-ruled areas of the body are primarily related to fluidity: these areas purify, balance, and release energy as well as receive positive energy. Use Pisces energy to connect to the broad spectrum of life, potential energy, intuition, mystical states, and creative imagination.

How grounding works

The practice of grounding is an activity that connects the Pisces-ruled feet to the Taurus-ruled Earth. The electro-magnetic energy field of both the Earth's atmosphere and your individual human aura are both shaped as toros fields, also phonetically related to Taurus. In the process of grounding, the Piscean energy channels in the feet connect your energy field directly to the Earth's energy field. In doing so, your personal auric field is cleansed by mother nature.

What is happening on a scientific level has to do with the electrical charge of your body taking in the negatively-charged antioxidants of the Earth to neutralize positively-charged pathogens causing inflammation.

To practice grounding, simply find a pleasant space to walk barefoot in nature. Grassy areas or sandy beaches tend to be good choices. Take note of how you're feeling both before and after practicing grounding.

♓ Pisces At-A-Glance	
Tropical Zodiac Solar Transit	February 19-March 20
Modality and Element	Mutable Water
Rulership	Neptune (Modern) Jupiter (Traditional)
Exaltation	Venus
Physical Connections	Feet, Lymphatic System
Chakra	Svadhisthana (Sacral)

Is This All You Need to Know About the Zodiac?

The zodiac is filled with symbols and mysteries that have been shared by the highest teachers in astrology, yoga, ancient mythologies, and spiritual systems. The words in this book are simply a starting point to take you beyond surface-level understanding of the zodiac and into the beginnings of the inner workings.

If you are diligent and persist in contemplating the zodiac, more truths will be revealed to you through synchronicities and elaboration through your subconscious. As time goes on, what I've written in these pages may seem obvious, as humanity more fully shifts into the Aquarian perspective.

Keep thinking about the zodiac. These signs will help you unlock energetic channels within yourself as well as develop a keen understanding of the world around you.

Chapter 6: The Zodiac, Planets, and the Subtle Body (Chakras, Koshas, Mudras)

Key Points in this Chapter
- The physical and subtle bodies are intrinsic to one another, yet are explored through disparate models to examine their particular functions.
- Chakras are energetic wheels in your form, and there are seven primary chakras along the energetic midline of your body. These correspond to the zodiac signs and planets.
- Koshas are energetic sheaths that correspond to predominating states that interact with one another to form layers of your consciousness. These correspond to the elements.
- Mudras are energetic seals that direct energy through the body. Hasta mudras are hand gestures that make use of acupressure points in the hands in order to produce particular energetic outcomes.

The Link of the Physical and Subtle

The physical body and subtle body are one. Even though the physical zodiac and the subtle body associations with astrology occur in separate chapters in this book, their unity should be considered central to the study of AstroYoga.

We tease out models of the subtle body and systems of the physical body in order to gain a more exact understanding of the specific properties and functions of each. But in truth, the physical body cannot be wholly divided from the subtle body. A more accurate understanding is to think of the physical as a layer of the subtle body, and one that is in a state of perpetual change.

For the purposes of AstroYoga, the subtle body is the energetic, spiritual aspect of the body. The subtle body is your body when predominantly considered according to its energetic characteristics, rather than its physical correspondences.

In earlier chapters, we've discussed how the three primary nadis of the body are associated with the luminaries. In this chapter we'll be getting into the chakras (energy wheels), the koshas (sheaths), and mudras (energetic seals) and what roles they play in AstroYoga.

Chakras

The model of the subtle body that has the greatest emphasis in pop culture, as well as inter-cultural prominence, is the chakra system. What we call chakras, or wheels, in yoga can be seen as the tree of life of the Cabalists, the seven metals of alchemy, the seven planets of traditional astrology, and the seven sacraments of esoteric Christianity.

That awakened beings from every culture have recognized the importance of the chakras illustrates that, though there are many words and languages to describe the truth of the Self, there is only one absolute truth. The system, language, or symbols you use approaching the highest truth are of no ultimate significance as long as they are accurate systems.

Take the time to understand some of the theory surrounding the chakras. This will lead to an understanding of the unification of the cosmos with the body and the truth of how the planets and zodiac behave at the human and human-spiritual levels of consciousness.

Muladhara

Muladhara chakra is the root chakra, which is located at the base of the spine near the perineum. Muladhara translates to root (mula) support (adhara), and it is associated with Saturn, Capricorn, Aquarius, and the earth element. As well, Mars is exalted in muladhara chakra.

Muladhara chakra relates to your capacity to feel safe and worthy of being embodied in your life. As is implied by the word muladhara, your ability to root down and to accept the support that is always available through the earth directly affects your sense of safety and self-worth.

This energy center is essential for recognizing that you not only deserve to be here in a fully embodied state, but that you are an integral part of the natural world. We think of ourselves as separate beings with individual identities; the root is the location that initially forms that individual identity.

Capricorn's presence in this chakra reminds us that physical forms are meant for purposeful, embodied action, and Aquarius' presence in this chakra demonstrates that we ultimately take on our individuality so as to be of service to others. To have form (Saturn) is natural here, but to initiate individual action in harmonious alignment with your own self actualization and selfless service is the highest form of this chakra, and is associated with Mars' exaltation in this chakra.

The symbol for muladhara chakra is a red lotus with four petals surrounding a square containing a downward-facing triangle. Here we see this chakra connects four main nadi channels that flow into it, and also understand that four represents a foundational number. The square represents the physical plane of existence. The number four also connects us to ideas of stability, personal dominion, and organizing yourself in such a way that you are calm and contented with your life.

Svadhisthana

Svadhisthana chakra is the sacral chakra, which is located near the center of the body, beneath the navel, where the womb is in women. Svadhisthana translates to self (sva) establishment or dwelling place (adhisthana), and it is associated with Jupiter, Sagittarius, Pisces, and the water element. As well, Venus is exalted in svadhisthana chakra.

Svadhisthana chakra relates to your capacity to experience states of joy, depth, and creativity. The self is most itself when moving in ways that create and spark joy, as is implied by the meaning of svadhisthana.

This energy center is essential for not only establishing joy, but for overcoming states of consciousness which keep you stuck. Anxiety, depression, greed, and worry can all come into play when svadhisthana is ignored. From the view of AstroYoga, true joy and creativity are essential for abiding as yourself. They are also key antidotes to the states of consciousness we call anxiety and depression.

Sagittarius' presence in this chakra implies that truly dwelling in the self will expand our personal consciousness, and Pisces' presence here connects to the truth that all creativity connects us to our true nature as an aspect of the eternally creative universe. Joy and creativity connect us to the freedom given by Truth (Jupiter), and this is what can help us to fall in love with ourselves (Venus). Venus' exaltation in this chakra demonstrates that true knowledge of the self translates to self love that begins to extend to all beings.

The symbol for svadhisthana chakra is an orange lotus with six petals surrounding a crescent or two concentric circles. Here we see this chakra connects six main nadis that flow into it, and also understand that six represents an energy of love, harmony, equilibrium, and beauty. The crescent symbolizes this chakra's relationship with water and with the cycles of time and experience. The energy here may help establish the personal self in a way that promotes health and harmony within, which inevitably spreads outward to bless those around you.

Manipura

Manipura chakra is the solar plexus chakra, which is located near the diaphragm. Manipura translates to jeweled (mani) city (pura) or the illustrious gem, and it is associated with Mars, Aries, Scorpio, and the fire element. As well, the Sun is exalted in manipura chakra and there is an esoteric association with Jupiter.

Manipura chakra relates to your capacity to digest, transform, and direct your experiences. It can help you direct the channels of prana in your body, and it also can act as a pressure valve that directs energy upward as it rises toward the crown.

This energy center is essential not just for directing energy, but also for building forms of energy. The manifest world has an endless number of ways for you to spend or build your energy, and manipura helps you wisely direct or contain your personal prana. To be able to direct your own power creates within you a sense of personal power and integrity. It also allows you to choose your reactions and responses, rather than act in anger or in heightened states of emotion.

Aries in this chakra represents the ability to act as you will, according to your well-reasoned intentions. Scorpio's presence here demonstrates manipura as a location that acts as a propulsion center for the rising energy through the nadis. This is one key point where Scorpio energy can act as the snake or rising force of kundalini, one of its key emblems.

Your ability to direct energy is the force of Mars at play in manipura, whereas this chakra's relationship to holding power and esteem connect it to the solar light manifesting as you. The Sun's exaltation here exemplifies that the right use of your personal allotment of solar energy is using your personal power in alignment with your highest will. Jupiter is at play here as well, connecting your capacity to direct your energy with your capacity to digest experiences in a way aligned with truth and personal empowerment.

The symbol for manipura chakra is a yellow lotus with ten petals around a downward-facing triangle. Here we see this chakra connects ten main nadis that flow into it, and also understand that ten represents an energy of the cosmic wheel of fortune in its specific emanation through you, an embodied being. Ten is also a number associated with Jupiter. The downward-facing triangle implies that it's best to align the lower forms of will and power with the highest Will of the universe. The energy here may help you contain and direct your energy that leads to the right use of power and the experience of personal empowerment.

Anahata

Anahata chakra is the heart chakra, which is located in the center of the body near the physical heart. Anahata translates to unstruck sound, unhurt, or unbeaten, and it is associated with Venus, Taurus, Libra, and the air element. As well, Saturn is exalted in anahata chakra.

Anahata chakra relates to your capacity to tap into the pure space of the heart, and to continue to follow your heart even when life places challenges in your path. Although the physical heart beats, the heart center is the one place that cannot be beaten down and from which pours the inner wisdom from the silent voice within, as both are implied by the meaning of anahata.

This chakra is at the center of your being, and is one of the seats of the personal soul. In the understanding of AstroYoga philosophy is the concept that the universe's intelligence is omnipotent, or present everywhere, centering itself in every being. This chakra is a primary access point to your personal connection with the larger intelligence of the universe itself. It is also the place you can go for healing and returning to a state of wholeness, since it can never be beaten down.

Taurus in this chakra relates to the realization that your being is an emanation of the love force universally present in nature. Libra's presence here demonstrates the reverberating resonance that your heart has with all other beings, since they are also emanations of the divine force of love. Venus' association with love is obvious here, and Saturn's connection with this chakra demonstrates both the necessary task of protecting the heart space as well as the realization that the purity of the heart's love is best experienced as a real presence in the structural reality of life.

The symbol for anahata chakra is a green lotus with twelve petals surrounding a hexagram star, or two triangles overlaying one another. Here we see this chakra connects twelve main nadis that flow into it, and also understand that twelve represents a perspective of seeing life through the eyes of love rather than attraction and aversion. Twelve is also a number of the totality of human experience from a place of inner wholeness. The hexagram star indicates balance, wholeness, and the joining of the superconscious aspects of self with the subconscious aspects of self.

Vishuddha

Vishuddha chakra is the throat chakra, which is located in the center of the neck. Vishuddha translates to very (vi) pure (shuddha or shuddhi), and is associated with Mercury, Gemini, Virgo, and the akasha/ether element. As well as being at home in this placement, Mercury is also in exaltation in vishuddha chakra.

Vishuddha chakra relates to your capacity to speak and listen from a place of clarity. This level of communication is associated with words that have immediate influence and effects of manifestation, and which tend to purify understanding, which is implied by the meaning of vishuddha.

This chakra is a space that transforms regular speech into utterances of mantra, where reality and your spoken words, written words, and thoughts align perfectly. This space relates to your capacity to hear and understand the voice of the heart or the inner teacher. There are energy centers surrounding this chakra that assist in connecting the higher centers of the brain with the shifts that occur as energy flows through the lower chakras. As well, this chakra is the source of subtle form of prana whose job is to purify toxins from the mind and body.

Gemini in this chakra relates to your capacity to choose your creation, thoughts, and words, as well as what you allow into your life. Virgo's presence here demonstrates the shifting nature of the material world through the agency of the mind. Mercury's relationship to this chakra demonstrates that thought can take either its lower form or its higher form, with the higher form being the very mechanism by which understanding, true wisdom, and authority over your own life experiences are possible.

The symbol for vishuddha chakra is a blue lotus with sixteen petals surrounding a downward-facing triangle with a circle inside it. Here we see this chakra connects sixteen primary nadis that flow into it, and also understand that sixteen represents the lightning flash that gives us glimpses to purified understanding. The triangle with the circle indicates the influx of superconscious energy that may be channeled into the body through this chakra.

Ajna

Ajna chakra is the third-eye chakra, which is located in the center of the skull. Ajna translates to authority, command, and perceive, and is associated with the Sun, Moon, Cancer, Leo, and light. As well, Jupiter is exalted in ajna chakra.

Ajna chakra relates to your capacity to clearly perceive life as well as command your body and your lived reality. Ajna chakra holds the lesson that it is your perception that writes your personal experience of life and that accurate perception grants true authority over your life. True authority implies being the author of your own story.

This chakra is a space that connects you beyond the ordinary levels of human living and elevates your experience to one of enlightenment. Ajna is the doorway to seeing all of the manifest world and unmanifest energy as emanations of the light of the universe.

Cancer in this chakra represents your ability to command the subconscious arenas of life, power, and manifestation. Leo's presence here relates to your capacity to identify with the superconscious level of life, rather than solely with the changeable ego-identity. The Sun and Moon represent this chakra's ability to connect and integrate all forms of light and consciousness, and Jupiter's exaltation here implies that the highest function of Jupiterian Truth is discovering and identifying yourself with the light of all reality.

The symbol for ajna chakra is an indigo lotus with two petals surrounding a downward-facing triangle containing an Om. Here we see this chakra connects two main nadis that flow into it, and also understand that two represents a perspective that you're still a distinct being who is acting under the command of your higher forms of consciousness. The triangle with the Om implies that an influx of unity consciousness may be channeled into the body through this chakra.

Sahasrara

Sahasrara chakra is the crown chakra, which is located at the crown, just above the skull. Sahasrara means thousand-petaled, and it is the whorl that connects the individuated sense of awareness with the higher chakras of consciousness that unite the single human awareness with the awareness of the universe. This chakra exists beyond the personal aspects of human personality known as the zodiac and instead abides in a state of unity, which ultimately passes into an awareness of the No-Thing.

The Chakras

Chakra	Zodiac Signs	Ruling Planet	Exalted Planet
Muladhara (Root)	Capricorn, Aquarius	Saturn	Mars
Svadhisthana (Sacral)	Sagittarius, Pisces	Jupiter	Venus
Manipura (Solar Plexus)	Aries, Scorpio	Mars	Sun
Anahata (Heart)	Taurus, Libra	Venus	Moon, Saturn
Vishuddha (Throat)	Virgo, Gemini	Mercury	Mercury
Ajna (Third Eye)	Leo, Cancer	Sun, Moon	Jupiter

At this point, try contemplating how the chakras relate to each other. The nadis connect the chakras, taking you through these predominating centers of consciousness. As you connect with and examine your chakras, you might notice that the misalignment of one chakra has the capacity to spread to the others. You might also notice that healthy expression in any one chakra will help support the healthy expression of other chakras.

For example, a fully embodied person whose Muladhara chakra connects them to the earth and those around them is more likely to feel worthy of experiencing the states of joy and creativity associated with Svadhisthana chakra. A truly joyful, creative person is likely to envision ways to use their energy optimally, which connects to a healthy Manipura chakra.

These chakras contain profound energy, and it's not advisable to force your chakras to open through extreme measures, such as the use of substances. Rather, you can work with your chakras by aligning your body and energy with the healthy flow of planetary influence. As with everything in AstroYoga, the rudimentary eventually translates to the mystical. The chakras are gateways to potent forms of consciousness that are always already alive in you, as you, and through you.

Examining Your Chakras with a Pendulum

The chakras have notable energetic fields that extend beyond the physical layer of the body. To learn more about how the energy is operating in your auric field extending from each chakra you may use a pendulum. Your pendulum doesn't need to be fancy—any object dangling from a single string or chain will do.

To examine your chakras, lie on your back (or stomach if you are examining the back chakras) and hold the pendulum above each chakra, one at a time. If the chakra energy is flowing smoothly, the pendulum will spin in a circle.

If the pendulum does not move, shakes, or moves in an erratic way, first double-check that you've held the pendulum above the proper chakra center. You may want a friend to help you. If you've definitely placed the pendulum well, measure the chakra output again in a few days, as sometimes chakra output differs according to rudimentary shifts, such as when you are tired or hungry.

The front chakras should have energy emanating from them, and the back chakras should have energy moving into them. If you discover a particular chakra is regularly not operating at a high level, you may take steps to organize your wellbeing surrounding the themes of that chakra. It's important to never directly attempt to manipulate the chakra to open (for example via the use of drugs), as this can cause damage.

Chakra tendencies can also be seen in the aspects of the astrology chart when you consider the astrological associations with the chakras in relationship to the dynamics of the chart, which will be explored in chapter seven.

Koshas

The koshas are the layers or sheaths of the subtle body. Like many subtle body models, the koshic model both includes and transcends the physical body. Physical embodiment paired with transcendental human aspects join together in the kosha system to serve as a reminder that our truest form is wholeness on every level, even though we can comprehend and study our disparate parts. In other words, enlightenment and bliss are meant to be experienced in the physical, now moment. An understanding of the koshas can drive you forward in your AstroYoga practice, particularly in the physical and subtle associations with the elements in the zodiac.

There are five koshas that are most often depicted as nestling into one another, like a set of nesting dolls, each contained by a larger sheath. This is a useful way to imagine these kosha layers, but consider that the sheaths could be envisioned as both small to large, and also large to small. You might also see that the koshic sheaths are interwoven with one another, each permeating the wholeness of your form.

Each kosha has its useful place in the wholeness of your being. When I teach the koshas, I'll often ask participants to reflect on times when they've favored one sheath, consciously moved from sheath to sheath, felt stuck within a sheath, or felt as though they couldn't access a particular sheath. As well, I ask them to consider what healthy energy would look like within each kosha. You might consider these topics as well.

Annamaya Kosha

Annamaya kosha translates to the food sheath, or your physical body. This kosha allows the senses to be used, and in astrology it corresponds to the earth element and Taurus, Virgo, and Capricorn.

A healthy use of annamaya kosha recognizes that though the physical body appears as solid in a moment, it is changeable in time, literally used as food for the energy systems in your form. Annamaya kosha is a place practitioners may become stuck if they over-focus on appearances or identify mainly with the perception of their body.

Pranamaya Kosha

Pranamaya kosha translates to the vital or energetic sheath. This kosha contains the vital energy that causes the body to have motion through means such as thirst, temperature regulation, and sexual excitement. Pranamaya kosha corresponds to the water element and Cancer, Scorpio, and Pisces.

A healthy use of pranamaya kosha balances input and output of energy in such a way that regulates a healthy physical and mental state. Spending too much energy can deplete the body, and containing too much energy can lead to a life purposely spent in isolation or suppression. Pranamaya kosha is a place practitioners may become stuck if they over-focus on external desires or aversions, rather than an inner state of equilibrium.

Manamaya Kosha

Manamaya kosha translates to the mental and sensing sheath. This kosha contains the part of you that thinks and feels, and in astrology it corresponds to the fire element and Aries, Leo, and Sagittarius.

A healthy use of manamaya kosha hones the mind, senses, and emotions to process information and experiences in an accurate way. This is possible when the desire/aversion nature in pranamaya kosha is in its place, as well as when you are fully present to make right impressions of the experiential world around and within you. Manamaya kosha is a place practitioners may become stuck if they have a tendency to get lost in their emotions or are given to rumination.

Vijnanamaya Kosha

Vijnanamaya kosha translates to the intellectual sheath. This kosha contains the part of you that has access to the higher potentials of reason and wisdom. This layer of the mind is more discerning than the changeable mental state of manamaya kosha. In astrology, vijnanamaya kosha corresponds to the air element and to Gemini, Libra, and Aquarius.

A healthy use of vijnanamaya kosha engages your rational mind to set your life in order. The truths present in wisdom are universal and may be applied to any situation. To access vijnanamaya kosha means to connect with wise counsel. This kosha is a place practitioners may become stuck if they have a tendency to intellectualize without applying thought into lived action.

Anandamaya Kosha

Anandamaya kosha translates to the bliss sheath. This sheath references the piece of the self that is pure consciousness. Anandamaya kosha is a microcosm, or personal subset, of the nature of spirit. In astrology, anandamaya kosha corresponds to the ether or akasha element, that which holds and permeates all things.

A healthy use of anandamaya kosha recognizes the presence of bliss in all aspects of your life, while simultaneously recognizing and engaging with your lived present moment. To access anandamaya kosha is to see that bliss lies in every step along the human journey, even in those experiences that seem paradoxic to bliss. Practitioners may become stuck in anandamaya kosha when they try to falsely access bliss through substances or numbing agents while in denial of their present reality.

The Koshas		
Kosha	Layer of Being	Element
Annamaya Kosha	Body	Earth
Pranamaya Kosha	Senses	Water
Manamaya Kosha	Emotion	Fire
Vijnanamaya Kosha	Intellect	Air
Anandamaya Kosha	Consciousness	Ether/Akasha

Hasta Mudras

A mudra is an energetic seal within the body. By sealing particular energetic pathways, mudras direct energy along the unsealed, freely flowing channels of the body. While there are large mudras that can be made with the full body (as in tarasana, star pose) or parts of the body (as in the bandha 'locks' at the root, thoracic diaphragm, and throat), here we'll be discussing hand mudras, or hasta mudras.

Despite there being many types of mudras, hasta mudras are the most well known, and they direct energy through the subtle channels (nadis) of the body, which are physically linked to both the fascial and nervous systems.

Before studying specific hasta mudras, take a moment to learn the connection between the hands and astrology.

Chapter 6: The Zodiac, Planets, and the Subtle Body (Chakras, Koshas, Mudras)

Astrology In Your Hands		
Hand Placement	Planet	Element
Thumb	Mars	Fire
Index Finger	Jupiter	Air
Middle Finger	Saturn	Ether
Ring Finger	Sun	Earth
Pinky Finger	Mercury	Water
Radial (Thumb) Mound	Venus	
Ulnar (Heel) Mound	Moon	

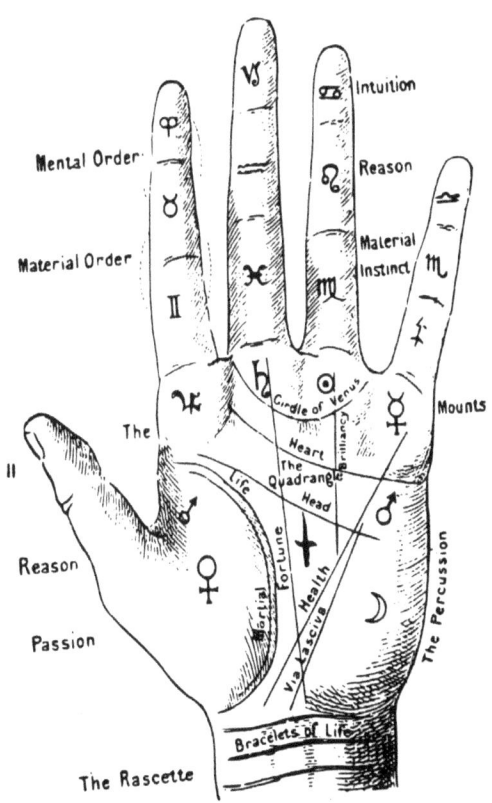

113

There are many mudras that can be made through the hands. It's beyond the scope of this book to examine every hasta mudra, but some common ones are listed below.

Anjali Mudra

Method: Place palms together in front of the heart.

This is the most common hasta mudra, and has a general outcome of reverence. This mudra serves to put the personality aside by sealing the channels of all zodiac elements and planets, placing them before the heart, which purifies and leads to higher degrees of consciousness.

Jnana Mudra

Method: Place pointer finger to thumb.

This is a common meditation mudra and takes the air finger to the fire finger. This has the effect of taking the airy mind and sealing it within the fire of meditation. Fire has the tendency to purify, so this is an ideal mudra for meditation in order to purify the qualities of the mind.

Prithivi Mudra

Method: Place the ring finger to thumb.

This mudra is used to aid digestion, increase vitality, and build joy. We see here that the earth element finger is purified through joining with the fiery thumb. Fire purifies earth to dispel outdated burdens and to infuse your body with energy, vitality, and joy.

Abhaya Mudra

Method: Place your open palm facing out from your shoulder.

This mudra is used to create a sense of courage and peace. When practicing this mudra, your energetic field opens and the center of the palm, which is a channel for the heart, shines out to meet what comes. This is a mudra of giving precedence to a particular channel, rather than completely sealing off passageways. As such, this mudra allows your current experience to be met with peace and strength. Many statues of deities hold this mudra.

Palmistry, reflexology, and acupressure have been popular in many cultures throughout history. As you study the topic of the connection between the hands and energy body, you may come across systems that initially appear to disagree with other systems. If the system is in tact (meaning it's effective), look more deeply. What at first glance appears as a paradox often contains many answers.

Practice:

Practice touching the four fingers, one by one, to the thumb. What do you notice when each finger pairs with the thumb? How do these pairings relate to the elements? How does your inner experience shift?

Subtle Body Astrology Work

The vastness of the subtle body and the many phenomena of consciousness that can't be put into words necessitate that the information in this chapter is merely a framework for understanding layers of human potential. There's so much more to explore from the topics discussed here. There are beings in every age who are fully enlightened and who have the capacity to use their bodies to the highest extent. However, at this stage, most people do not have that capacity realized, even though the potential for complete illumination exists in every person.

What modern scientists consider 'junk DNA,' neurological ganglia too complex to define, and unused brain cells are actually key biological correspondences to the subtle body phenomena. Your biology activates as greater states of enlightenment take root in your form.

Subtle body models are roadmaps to help you understand what is taking hold in your physical being as more and more of your DNA starts to activate and come online. Human beings are both natural and cultural: we have a natural body that is ours to develop through the progression of our own consciousness on the road to greater enlightenment. This is the meaning of the 'great work' that is often referred to. Your very form and consciousness are your personal magnum opus.

As you work with your subtle body, take an approach that is safe, repeatable, and easily tracked as to its effectiveness. There are many such yoga practices that fit this bill. As you continue on your path, take note as to what shifts you notice in your consciousness, your physiology, and your energy. These shifts tend (though not always) to occur slowly over time. Look back at any five year stretch of intense yogic practice and see how far you've come.

Chapter 7: Houses, Aspects, and Reading the Natal Chart

Key Points in this Chapter
- AstroYoga practice is enhanced by accurate chart interpretation.
- Houses in astrology charts mark arenas of life that relate to the signs and planets in particular ways.
- In the Aquarian Age, the energetic emphasis of the houses shifts from the energetic emphasis in the Piscean Age.
- Aspects in astrology allow you to read the energetic relationship among planets in the natal chart.
- Reading astrology charts is a natural step in the study of AstroYoga.

Essential Knowledge for Chart Interpretation

This is not a book on natal chart interpretation, though I imagine many of the concepts in this book will enhance any chart interpretations you may offer, should you choose to go that route. Many books on the basics of chart interpretation exist, and it's not my intention to reproduce information that's already easily and widely available in both the tropical and sidereal approaches to interpretation.

Nevertheless, natal chart interpretation is relevant to the study of AstroYoga, so gaining proficiency in interpretation naturally accompanies a study of this field.

When interpreting the natal chart, it's essential to view it as a map, as well as a crystalline grid of information relevant to the being it describes. In the next few pages, I'll go into a brief discussion of the houses and aspects, and also offer a general guide to assist with reading astrology charts.

Houses

When you're examining an astrology chart, the areas where the planets and zodiac are placed are called the houses. Houses represent the arena of life in which the chart placements operate. While the houses aren't given as much attention as the zodiac, they still warrant deep contemplation when it comes to chart interpretation.

Like the zodiac, the houses are twelve in number. They have a natural connection with the zodiac signs and their rulerships and exaltations. These natural associations run from Aries through Pisces, houses one through twelve respectively.

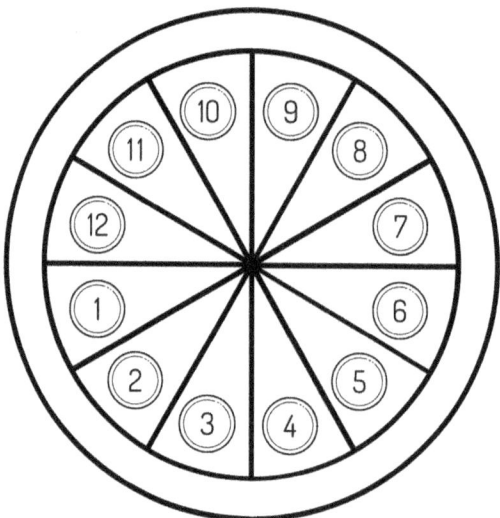

Like the zodiac, the houses can be divided by qualities, or examined one-by-one as a narrative structure of life.

The first and easiest way to consider the houses is as a cycle of energy: a metaphoric birth-through-death cycle of existence. Each house generally rules an arena of life that we all experience. When you examine your chart, consider what your experiences are in each house.

The flow of narrative and cyclical energy moves in the following way:

In the first house we emerge as an individual being with an individual purpose. We have specified ourselves from the unmanifest field of potentiality in the etherial waters. For this reason the first house rules the experience and expression of self. The natural zodiac placement in the first house is Aries.

In the second house we define ourselves further by articulating our values and discovering the tools which we possess. For this reason the second house rules personal values, finances, and possessions. The natural zodiac placement in the second house is Taurus.

In the third house we encounter our local environment, peer group, and the opinions of those around us. For this reason the third house rules learning, siblings, and opinion formation. The natural zodiac placement in the third house is Gemini.

In the fourth house we are nurtured into the beings we are in our roots, and we gain deeper understanding of life through our family and home environment. For this reason the fourth house rules psychic depths and the home. The natural zodiac placement in the fourth house is Cancer.

In the fifth house we express play and creativity. If the first four houses have provided a sufficiently safe and nurturing space, then in the fifth house we play from a place of joy. If traumas have taken place, then the fifth house can be a place where transgressive play is used to process life thus far. Most people experience a combination of these fifth house factors. For this reason the fifth house rules play, creativity, and debauchery. The natural zodiac placement in the fifth house is Leo.

In the sixth house we form our habits of daily routine, hygiene, health, and work. Ideally, these habits are born from the fifth house and what we genuinely enjoy and want to create. For this reason the sixth house rules health and work. The natural zodiac placement in the sixth house is Virgo. The sixth house is particularly important for those who want to use AstroYoga as a primary wellness practice.

In the seventh house we take our individual experiences and begin to tie ourselves to others in relationship. For this reason the seventh house rules significant relationships and partnerships. The natural zodiac placement in the seventh house is Libra.

In the eighth house we complicate our relationships by sharing our psychic roots as well as our material possessions. We dig in deep and see the gifts we bring to each other, our similarities, and our differences. For this reason the eighth house rules shared values and possessions, as well as those life instances where money is inherited or shared (birth, death, marriage, divorce). The natural zodiac placement in the eighth house is Scorpio.

In the ninth house we explore the depths of the eighth house by exploring the world at large in terms of travel, higher education, philosophy, and religion. For this reason the ninth house rules anything that expands the mind or belief system. The natural zodiac placement in the ninth house is Sagittarius.

In the tenth house we take all that we've learned so far and put ourselves 'out there' in the world. Our work grows into a career, or we take our various roles out in society as businesspeople, parents, hobbyists, etc. For this reason the tenth house rules reputation, fame, and career. The natural zodiac placement in the tenth house is Capricorn.

In the eleventh house we take all that we are in society and begin to think of how it can serve those beyond ourselves. We innovate, commune with others, and envision a society where life's most burning questions are solved and beings everywhere are happy and free. For this reason the eleventh house rules community and innovation. The natural zodiac placement in the eleventh house is Aquarius.

In the twelfth house we let go of our say in matters and take a more experiential, spiritual view of reality. We begin to flow into the oneness of all, letting go of individuation in order to once more experience the universal. For this reason the twelfth house rules spirituality, dissolution, and unity. The natural zodiac placement in the twelfth house is Pisces.

The Houses in Pairs

Each house can be paired with its opposite to see a spectrum of arenas in life that can open us to experiencing the new or the familiar, the personal or the interpersonal. In brief, they are:

Houses One and Seven

These houses assert who you are in house one, and then call who you are into reflection through relationships in house seven.

Houses Two and Eight

These houses assert your values and possessions in house two, and then call your values and finances into reflection through the realization of what you share with others and what others have shared with you in house eight.

Houses Three and Nine

These houses determine what you've learned and how you think and communicate in house three, and then test your beliefs against universal truth in house nine.

Houses Four and Ten

These houses nourish you in the privacy of the home in house four, and then bring your inner self into the outer world to be known publicly in house ten.

Houses Five and Eleven

These houses allow you to play and create for yourself in house five, and then offer your unique creativity into the world for your community in house eleven.

Houses Six and Twelve

These houses build your health, work, and daily habits through what's specific in house six, and then release routine and specificity for the spiritual, artistic, and universal in house twelve.

The Houses in Threes

The houses may be divided into groups that correspond to the natural placement of the zodiac when grouped by elements. These house groupings highlight particular themes in life. In brief, they are:

Spirit (Fire) Houses: One, Five, and Nine

These houses connect self in house one with what you create in house five and how you expand your sense of self in house nine. All of these houses have a central connection to play and how you know yourself and place yourself in the world.

Material (Earth) Houses: Two, Six, and Ten

These houses connect you to the material in house two with what you do in house six and how you appear to others over time in house ten. All of these houses have a central connection to what is built over time and where your values truly stand.

Relational (Air) Houses: Three, Seven, and Eleven

These houses connect you to the formation of early relationships in house three to the cultivation of significant partnerships or marriage in house seven to the interconnectivity of community in house eleven. All of these houses have a central connection to who you are in relationship to others.

Soul (Water) Houses: Four, Eight, and Twelve

These houses connect you to the individual soul in house four to the familial soul in house eight to the oneness of all souls in house twelve. All of these houses have a central connection to the spiritual and interconnected sense of self through space, time, and dimensions.

The Houses in Fours

The houses may be divided into groups that correspond to the natural placement of the zodiac when grouped by quadruplicity. These house groupings highlight the actionability or reactivity of particular arenas of life. In brief, they are:

The Angular Houses: One, Four, Seven, and Ten

The angular houses correspond to the cardinal placements of the natural zodiac and represent initiatory arenas of life, which move you: into the self in house one; into the roots of life in house four; into relationships in house seven; and into the public in house ten. The angular houses tend to move a person forward.

The Succedent Houses: Two, Five, Eight, and Eleven

The succedent houses correspond to the fixed placements of the natural zodiac and represent the sustained arenas of life: sustained personal values in house two; sustained creative energy in house five; sustained connection to family in house eight; and sustained community involvement in house eleven. The succedent houses tend to sustain a person and ground them in what is consistent in life.

The Cadent Houses: Three, Six, Nine, and Twelve

The cadent houses correspond to the mutable placements in the natural zodiac and represent that which changes in life and prepares us for growth: changing opinions and locations in house three; changing habits and work dynamics in house six; changing philosophies and worldviews in house nine; and changing experiences of the universe and spirituality in house twelve. The cadent houses tend to shift people and help them grow to reconcile seemingly disparate aspects of themselves.

Additional House Groupings

I have listed the primary ways the houses are examined and grouped, but there are more. The circle can be divided in quadrants, halves, and thirds. The following discussion on the aspects will help you know when and how to examine these house relationships.

Houses and the Aquarian Age

I titled this book *Astro Yoga for an Aquarian Age* because we are at the dawning of a new age in which the secrecy often associated with keener understandings of these systems is meant to be practiced openly. To be sure, there will always be those secrets that cannot be written because language fails to express their potency. Yet in this age, integrative knowledge, as well as spiritual integration in the physical, are meant to be accessible to all.

One measure determining astrological ages is where the vernal equinox falls along the sidereal, constellatory zodiac. In tropical time, the spring equinox marks zero degrees Aries, but in sidereal time, the equinox point during the Aquarian Age falls into the sign of Aquarius. During this age, the houses can be thought of as being associated with both their natural sign (Aries through Pisces, corresponding to houses one through twelve), as well as their Aquarian layout (Aquarius through Capricorn, also corresponding to houses one through twelve).

We are entering the Aquarian Age and leaving the Piscean Age, the hallmark of which was religious influence, control, loss of control, and escape. At various moments, the lives from the Piscean Age both demonstrated the potential hardships and atrocities possible within this energetic structure, as well as displayed the higher vibrational ways this energy could be utilized. Everything that happened in the last 2000 years was a development within the energetic structure of the Piscean Age.

A Brief Overview of the Houses Against an Aquarian Backdrop

House One in Aquarius

The natural zodiac places Aries in house one because the cardinal spark of fire initiates knowledge of the self. In the Aquarian zodiac, the first house has the added layer of knowing ourselves through community, self-inquiry, and the body of wisdom accessible to us when we still our minds.

The Natural (Aries-Pisces) House Structure

The Aquarian (Aquarius-Capricorn) House Structure

House Two in Pisces

The natural zodiac places Taurus in house two because the fixed quality of earth holds and sustains values and material resources. In the Aquarian zodiac, the second house has the added layer of seeing material wealth as ephemeral and knowing that personal values and material goods need to align with our inspired experience of the universe at large.

House Three in Aries

The natural zodiac places Gemini in house three because the mutable quality of air allows the swiftness of mind to receive and give communications necessary to form opinions and keep everyday life going. In the Aquarian zodiac, the third house has the added layer of allowing the personal spark of spirit to drive opinion formation and relationships with others. Relationships will be more harmonious when we let ourselves be fully seen.

House Four in Taurus

The natural zodiac places Cancer in house four because the energy of nurture and care is the root of all matters of the soul and home. In the Aquarian zodiac, the fourth house has the added layer of allowing the height of beauty and richness to abide in the personal placement of soul. Good things will happen when richness and longevity are considered essential to the home space and personal root.

House Five in Gemini

The natural zodiac places Leo in house five because the fixed quality of fire in our hearts is what drives the creative process. In the Aquarian zodiac, the fifth house has the added layer of mental acuity and the ability to create quickly using the powers of the mind.

House Six in Cancer

The natural zodiac places Virgo in house six because of the detail-oriented nature of habits, hygiene, and daily work. Also these are areas over which we have some degree of control. In the Aquarian zodiac, the sixth house has the added layer of nurture in our work and habits, as well as an association with a feminine-encoded way of flowing through the work day. Hierarchical forms of work and scheduling make way for circadian work schedules.

House Seven in Leo

The natural zodiac places Libra in house seven because good partnerships require mental balance, commitment, love, action, and reaction. In the Aquarian zodiac, the seventh house has the added layer of heart-connection and spiritual alignment, essential in all marriages and partnerships.

House Eight in Virgo

The natural zodiac places Scorpio in house eight because depth and sharing resources with others requires a watery, deep commitment to spending energy in complementary ways. In the Aquarian zodiac, the eighth house has the added layer of controlling and rearranging energy in order to optimize interpersonal connection, create group spiritual awakenings, and rewrite/heal epigenetic traumas.

House Nine in Libra

The natural zodiac places Sagittarius in house nine because higher education, travel, and broadening horizons require the swirling, passionate energy of spirit. In the Aquarian zodiac, the ninth house has the added layer of balancing the familiar and unfamiliar and seeking the spiritual in all that can be experienced, thereby modifying past karmas and timelines of separation.

House Ten in Scorpio

The natural zodiac places Capricorn in house ten because career and reputation are formed with the steady directional movement of practical actions made over time. In the Aquarian zodiac, the tenth house has the added layer of depth in order to heal and create from a soul-centered space within careers. This soul-aligned quality will be the hallmark of careers in this timespan.

House Eleven in Sagittarius

The natural zodiac places Aquarius in house eleven because adding to community requires thinking outside the box and giving consideration to the swirling soul energies of individuals, along with the collective. In the Aquarian zodiac, the eleventh house has the added layer of spirituality and philosophy in the ways we relate to one another in community. Groups will gather around broader philosophical beliefs and the associative connection with those ideas.

House Twelve in Capricorn

The natural zodiac places Pisces in house twelve because spirituality and dissolution require the release of personal control in order to open to what is hiding in plain sight. In the Aquarian zodiac, the twelfth house has the added layer of steadily remembering what was once known by the mystics of astrology and yoga. Spirituality will require the connection of the past, present, and future in such a way that sees time for the particular dimension it is.

Aspects

The aspects are the relationships among planets, luminaries, and other objects in the zodiac. Each aspect has a particular character that is expressed through the relationship among the celestial objects involved. Being able to read aspects is one of the skills that will take you from amateur to professional status. I feel compelled to remind you that as you're learning, amateur status is the perfect place to be. The word amateur means a person who does something for the love of it, so never lose that amateur urge. Nevertheless, reading aspects will take your reading up a level, and tends to be one of the deciding factors in whether an astrologer is ready to professionally offer readings.

What follows are the basics you'll need to accurately interpret the relationships among objects in the chart and the body.

> **A Note on Aspect Orbs:** Not all aspects occur at the exact mathematical degree indicated. When interpreting charts, you will need to determine an aspect orb. You have a few options here:
>
> Beginner: Use the default in your preferred astrology software or website, or use a three degree orb.
>
> Intermediate: Use an aspect orb that is reasonable, but measured for type of aspects, such as eight degrees for conjunctions, five degrees for squares and trines, and three degrees for minor aspects. Interpret aspects as loose or close.
>
> Advanced: Understand that each degree point slightly shifts meaning, so read aspects with your artistic and mathematical mind applying an understanding of nuance in degree.

Conjunction

The conjunction is the circle divided by one. Anything divided by one is simply the same; conjunctions occupy the same place in the zodiac. In a conjunction, the energies of the placements merge, and they may not be able to be entirely differentiated from one another. Impacts made between these placements will be direct.

Opposition

The opposition is the circle divided by two. In an opposition, the energies of the placements occupy two sides of one spectrum in polarity. This can be experienced as a dance of polarity, a teeter-totter, or a tug-of-war, depending on the placements and the individual's ability to reconcile opposites. In an opposition, a person may choose one placement over the other, if culturally conditioned to favor one expression. It's healthiest to reconcile this if it has occurred.

Trine

The trine is the circle divided by three. In a trine, the energy flows easily and automatically among placements of the same element. The trine is experienced as ease, and often the individual is considered lucky in the particular element. If other placements in the chart do not offer sufficient challenge, the individual can become lazy. It's best for people with a significant number of trines to form definite goals in order to have a container for their blessings to flow into.

Square

The square is the circle divided by four. In a square, the energies encounter paradox and friction, as two energies move in similar ways but through different elements. The square aspect requires the individual to reconcile an inner paradox and face frustrations with equanimity. When this is done skillfully, massive growth is possible in the areas of the square.

Sextile

The sextile is the circle divided by six. In a sextile, the energies harmonize in such a way that encourages growth as complementary elements and quadruplicities come together. The sextile aspect tends to create an area where the individual is well-rounded.

> Listed above are only the major aspects. There are additional minor aspects which dedicated astrologers will devote some attention to. They are:
> - Semi-Sextile (The circle divided by 12 or 30 degrees)
> - Semi-Square (The circle divided by 8 or 45 degrees)
> - Sesquiquadrate (3/8 of a circle or 135 degrees)
> - Quincunx or Inconjunct (5/12 of a circle or 150 degrees)
> - Biquintile (2/5 of a circle or 144 degrees)
> - Quintile (The circle divided by five or 72 degrees)

It's worth taking time to learn the geometry of shapes within circles in enough detail that the mathematical and numerological implications of these degrees contain some meaning for you. Some minor aspects have a less obvious influence on the birth chart, yet contain deep esoteric meanings and implications for the individual's broader purpose in the universe. In particular, it's worth paying attention to the Quincunx relationship among planets, as it opens many doors to understanding what we misunderstand within ourselves.

Aspect Patterns

Sometimes aspects will arrange themselves in particular formations known as aspect patterns. A few of the more common aspect patterns are listed here, and more will be found with a deeper journey into the relationships among aspects within astrology and your body.

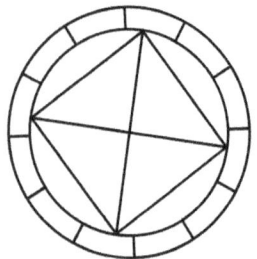

The Grand Cross

The grand cross is a formation made up of two oppositions which are square to one another. As its name implies, it forms a cross. Energetically, this can feel like a crossroad as well as a cross to bear. Grand crosses create a state of paradox within an individual that challenges them to articulate themselves in nuanced and specific ways.

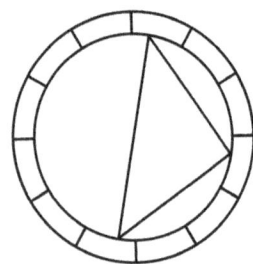

The T Square

T squares are similar to grand crosses, but T squares are made up of an opposition with a third placement squaring the opposition, forming a right triangle. Energetically, this can appear as alternating between building energy in a paradoxical place that feels sticky and moving with great speed and vigor once the paradox has been reconciled. T squares offer motivation and achievement when used well.

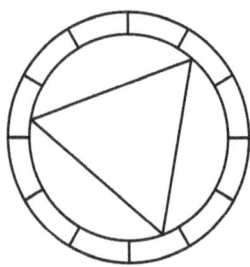

The Grand Trine

The grand trine is a formation made up of three placements trining one another, forming an equilateral triangle. Energetically, this can manifest in natural talent in the element of those trines. The energy flows freely and naturally, so the individual needs to be careful to use personal talents toward an aim, and not to allow those natural gifts to create aimlessness.

Chapter 7: Houses, Aspects, and Reading the Natal Chart

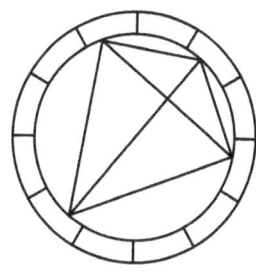

Kite

The kite formation is a grand trine with an additional sextile involved. Energetically, this pattern behaves similarly to the grand trine, but rounds it out a bit, allowing for an additional layer of depth and focus in the smooth-flowing energy of the trine. For the individual, this translates to luck that is directed toward a particular aim.

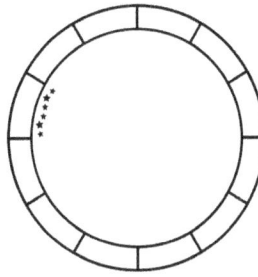

Stellium

Stellium means cluster of stars, and as a formation it indicates a cluster of placements in the same sign or house. Energetically, this creates an emphasis in a particular area of the chart, where major life gifts and challenges can play out. For the individual, this stellium influence occurs both in the sequential structure of time and also simultaneously in every moment.

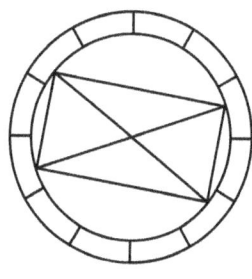

Mystic Rectangle

A mystic rectangle consists of four placements that form a rectangle with two sextiles and two oppositions. Energetically, this engages inner tension in a way that offers harmony and resolution. For the individual, this translates to talent and awareness in integrating inner paradox, as well as rapid personal growth in this lifetime.

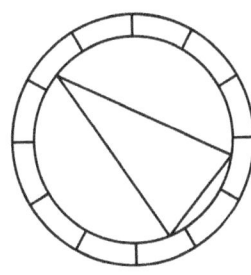

Yod

A Yod formation consists of two placements sextile to one another, with both quincunx to a third placement. Yod is the quintessential letter of the Hebrew 'flame' alphabet, and the formation looks much like this letter. Energetically, a Yod tends to manifest as a mission which requires one to overcome adversity. The Yod pattern forms a directional movement of energy in the chart.

How to Read an Astrology Chart

In most cases, the chart you'll be reading is a birth or natal chart. The skills used in reading and interpreting a natal chart are similar to those used when doing synastry (partnership), transit, progressed, solar return, and relocation readings. The first step is learning to read a birth chart, and the second step is practicing so you read the birth chart accurately and well.

With the previous chapters on the zodiac and planets, you already have many of the necessary skills needed to begin or continue reading birth charts.

The general flow of reading a birth chart is this:

- Make key decisions. Are you going to use tropical or sidereal time? What house system are you going to use? Are you interpreting the nine traditional planets, or are you adding in outer planets, asteroids, or other mathematical points? Note: If you are unsure where to begin, I suggest reading a tropical chart using the Placidus house structure and incorporating the original nine planets, outer planets, and Chiron.
- Look at the chart. What do you notice? Are the planets evenly spaced or clumped together? Do you see any notable patterns (whether you remember the names of all the aspect patterns or not)? Does the chart favor a particular element or quadruplicity? Are there planets near to any of the cardinal points or house cusps? Are any planets in their exaltation, domicile, or mutual reception (two planets in each other's domiciles)?
- Examine the simple implications of each planet, sign, and house placement. Note: This is what computer program print-outs will do for you, and while computer interpretations have value, the value of human interpretation lies in the next step.
- Paint the picture. Take the rudimentary interpretations from step three and read between the aspect lines to paint the picture of how the various tendencies, drives, and desires of the person interact with one another. Get a clear picture of how these energies flow in both high vibrational and low vibrational ways relative to the person, as well as how the energies manifest internally and externally.
- Add layers. Look at the current transits and their effect on the chart. Also as appropriate, layer on progressions, solar return or locational charts, or alternate modes of time.

Chart interpretation gets easier the more you do it. At first, you may miss some information or feel confused by the large amount of information present in symbolic language. Don't be discouraged! Mastery in chart interpretation comes with practice. Simply practice reading with good intentions and a clear foundation in the basics. You'll notice big shifts in your proficiency with time and practice.

Chapter 8: Planning Your AstroYoga Practice

Key Points in this Chapter
- Planning your AstroYoga practice should take into account how you already practice and/or teach.
- AstroYoga can be used to integrate natal chart placements, align with goals, or integrate particular transits.
- When working with postural yoga, the zodiac signs align with certain physical principles of practice.
- Certain planets, elements, and signs indicate particular types of practices.

Selecting Suitable AstroYoga Practices

After years of teaching this material, I've found that most people have one of two reactions after completing an in-depth study of AstroYoga. Either they take inspiration from what they've learned and begin to apply it with ease, or more commonly, they are not quite sure where to begin. After all, there are many layers of understanding within the complexities of AstroYoga, and these layers of understanding must be applied to the already complex task of planning appropriate yoga practices.

For the purpose of this chapter, I'll assume that you already have some level of understanding about the practice techniques or teaching techniques common to many modern practitioners of yoga. If you're unfamiliar with a particular yogic topic in this chapter, an easy search on the internet or chat with your yoga teacher will bring you up to speed.

The first thing to understand is that not every form of yoga practice is appropriate to every person. Personal factors such as age, ability, distinct needs, lifestyle, experience level, and personal demeanor should be taken into account. While every practice within yoga won't be suitable for every practitioner, every practitioner will be able to find some practices that are suitable to help them integrate their chart while practicing in alignment with the current transits. Take into account what the individual does for yoga practice. For example, some people exclusively practice physical, asana-based yoga, while others prefer to focus on breathwork and meditation. Of those who practice physically, some are seeking rigorous practice and others seek soothing practice. There are mantra yoga practices, mudra practices, and practices that combine various methods within yoga. Make sure your understanding is as well-informed as possible so you are operating within the highest integrity of practice available to you.

As well, decide what you will focus on before planning a practice for yourself or others. Those people will form practices focused on the energy of that placement, which also take into consideration energies aspecting that placement. Other people may simply want a well-balanced AstroYoga practice that integrates their chart to create a sense of personal alignment and long-term cohesion. Still others might be aware of how the transits are affecting their charts and will want to flow for that.

If the practice being created is for a group, it is advisable to form sequences based on the current planetary transits. Make sure you're designing practices in harmonious alignment with each transit, so as to work with, rather than fight against, the currents of energy.

Some basic guidelines to observe when planning your AstroYoga practice:

- Keep in mind the zodiac relationship to the body. Know how the systems of the body work, and have knowledge of the effect certain yoga practices have on the various physical systems, particularly in relationship to organs, endocrine glands, lymph, and the parasympathetic/sympathetic nervous system responses. This will help you know which practices align with which astrology placements.
- Keep in mind who the planets are and what their primary actions are in the body, mind, and personality. This will help you know what kind of energy you need to call on to practice in an aligned way.
- Keep in mind the themes present in the chakras and koshas as they relate to the zodiac and elements. These will present themes of consciousness that will arise in various forms of practice.
- On new and full moon days, do not practice rigorous, solar-encoded asana. Instead, practice predominantly lunar-encoded asana.
- Avoid practicing asana during eclipses. Instead practice meditation and japa.

- Follow the dictum of stabilized engagement during Chiron transits. Because Chiron is the wounded healer, it's important to stabilize and use body parts with an extra emphasis on holistic wellbeing during these transits.
- Include more meditation during retrogrades, as well as longer savasanas, if possible.
- Hold awareness of the higher potencies (discussed in chapters five and six) of the planetary and zodiac energies and seek to embody their highest expression.

Above all else, recognize that yoga as a system is intelligently constructed in alignment with astrology. If you know something is a sound yoga practice, and it is cohesive with your intelligently-constructed sequence, you'll probably find that it is in alignment with the transits.

What follows are some guideline practices that you can adapt to suit your personal needs or the needs of your yoga students. Keep in mind that designing a home-practice will differ from designing a studio-practice, similar to the way simple at-home cooking differs from creating restaurant fare for others. For at-home practice, it's recommended to keep it simple, with the understanding that you can always add transitions or additions that come to you in the moment. For a curated studio flow, you'll design transitions that keep the class focused in the moment and match your class style.

Understanding Asana as Related to the Zodiac

While the planets indicate the type of practice suitable to the characters of particular people or moments in time, most physical postures should be considered in relationship to the zodiac and its correspondence with the physical and subtle body. What follows is a brief breakdown of types of physical yoga suitable to the various zodiac signs. Postures may be applied to the signs that either invigorate or balance and soothe particular energies. Please keep in mind these are for illustration purposes, and an individual's distinct needs may require modifications or alternate practices that move along the zodiac themes. As well, please note that at the end of physical practice, all zodiac sign placements will benefit from the integrative practice of savasana.

Aries

Poses that direct energy through the head are applicable for Aries. To invigorate Aries energy, practice sirsasana (headstand) or sasangasana (rabbit pose). To soothe Aries energy, practice balasana (child's pose). Ideally, if you practice headstand, you'll practice child's pose with it. Any poses that support the function of the brain may be practiced when working with Aries energy.

♈	Sample Postures for Aries Energy
Sirsasana (Headstand)	
	Sasangasana (Rabbit Pose)
Balasana (Child's Pose)	

Taurus

Poses that move energy through the neck are applicable for Taurus. To invigorate Taurus energy, practice sarvangasana (shoulder stand). To balance Taurus energy, practice matsyasana (fish posture). Ideally, these two poses will be practiced together. Any poses that support the nervous, limbic, or endocrine system functions connected with the neck may be practiced when working with Taurus energy.

Gemini

Poses that circulate energy through the shoulders, hands, arms, and nervous system are applicable for Gemini. To invigorate Gemini energy, practice adho mukha svanasana (downward-facing dog) or kakasana (crow pose). To soothe Gemini energy, try baddha virabhadrasana (humble warrior). Any poses that support the function of the nervous system and promote wrist and shoulder health may be practiced when working with Gemini energy.

Sample Postures for Gemini Energy	
Kakasana (Crow Pose)	
	Adho Mukha Svanasana (Downward Facing Dog)
Baddha Virabhadrasana (Humble Warrior)	

Cancer

Poses that direct energy through the chest and stomach are applicable for Cancer. To invigorate Cancer energy, practice setubandhasana (bridge pose). To soothe Cancer energy, practice pashchimottanasana (seated forward fold). Any poses that support the healthy function and balance of the breasts and stomach may be practiced when working with Cancer energy.

Leo

Poses that move energy through the spine and open the heart are applicable for Leo. To invigorate Leo energy, practice backbends such as ustrasana (camel pose) or urdhva dhanurasana (upward-facing bow). To soothe Leo energy, practice tarasana (star pose). Any poses that support the wellbeing of the spine and heart may be practiced when working with Leo energy.

♌ Sample Postures for Leo Energy	
Ustrasana (Camel Pose)	
	Urdhva Dhanurasana (Upward-Facing Bow)
Tarasana (Star Pose)	

Virgo

Poses that circulate energy through digestive organs are applicable for Virgo. To invigorate Virgo energy, practice parivrtta anjaneyasana (twisted lunge) or a seated twist such as matsyendrasana (lord of the fishes pose). To soothe Virgo energy, practice supta vajrasana (reclining thunderbolt pose). Any poses that support the body's ability to digest food and experiences may be practiced when working with Virgo energy.

♍	Sample Postures for Virgo Energy
Parivrtta Anjaneyasana (Twisted Lunge)	
	Matsyendrasana (Lord of the Fishes Pose)
Supta Vajrasana (Reclining Thunderbolt Pose)	

Libra

Poses that move energy through the low back and support balance in kidney function are applicable for Libra. To invigorate Libra energy, practice vrksasana (tree pose). To soothe Libra energy, practice a marjaiasana-bitilasana (cat-cow) sequence. Any poses that support the functioning of the kidneys and balance the adrenals may be practiced when working with Libra energy.

Scorpio

Poses that build energy along the energetic channels of the body are applicable for Scorpio. To invigorate Scorpio energy, practice garudasana (eagle pose) or malasana (garland pose). To soothe Scorpio energy, practice baddha konasana (bound angle pose). Any poses that support the conscious direction of the life force and health of the pelvic floor may be practiced when working with Scorpio energy.

♏ Sample Postures for Scorpio Energy	
Garudasana (Eagle Pose)	
	Malasana (Garland Pose)
Baddhakonasana (Bound Angle Pose)	

Sagittarius

Poses that circulate energy through the hips and thighs are applicable for Sagittarius. To invigorate Sagittarius energy, practice virabhadrasana II (warrior two pose) or akarna dhanurasana (archer pose). To soothe Sagittarius energy, practice kapotasana (pigeon pose). Any poses that support proper function, strength, or energetic release in the hips, thighs, and quadriceps may be practiced when working with Sagittarius energy.

Capricorn

Poses that direct energy through the skeletal system are applicable for Capricorn. To invigorate Capricorn energy, practice utkatasana (chair pose). To soothe Capricorn energy, practice tadasana (mountain pose). Any poses that support the proper function of the knees or the proper structure of the bones may be practiced when working with Capricorn energy.

Aquarius

Poses that move energy through the ankles and blood are applicable for Aquarius. To invigorate Aquarius energy, practice adho mukha svanasana (downward-facing dog) or natarajasana (king dancer). To soothe Aquarius energy, practice a seated crosslegged pose such as padmasana (lotus pose). Any poses that support the circulatory system or strengthen the ankles may be practiced when working with Aquarius energy.

Sample Postures for Aquarius Energy	
Adho Mukha Svanasana (Downward-Facing Dog)	
	Natarajasana (King Dancer)
Padmasana (Lotus Pose)	

Pisces

Poses that circulate energy through the feet and lymph are applicable for Pisces. To invigorate Pisces energy, practice vajrasana on your toes (thunderbolt pose with the toes tucked under). To soothe Pisces energy, practice viparita karani (placing the legs up the wall) or ananda balasana (happy baby pose). Any poses that support the function of the lymphatic system or strengthen/massage the feet may be practiced when working with Pisces energy.

Solar and Lunar Flows

In general, solar flows are more heating, uplifting, directional, and active, while lunar flows are more cooling, grounding, cyclical, and passive. Each practice will necessarily contain aspects of the other, but one will predominate.

Solar flows tend to be scions of the sun salute, and often incorporate vinyasa. The word vinyasa means 'to apply to the body in a particular way,' yet modern yoga tends to use this word to describe the plank-chatturanga-up-dog-down-dog sequence. What is important in solar flows is the understanding that you are infusing the body with sunlight that has taken the form of breath and heat.

> There are several sacred associations with the number 108 in yoga. One such association is linguistic, since the matrika malini (translated as the garland of little mothers, the matrika malini is the Sanskrit alphabet) contains 54 letters, each with a masculine and feminine vibration (54 + 54 = 108). Another connection to the number 108 is astrological, since the nine original planets (Sun, Moon, Mercury, Venus, Mars, Jupiter, Saturn, Rahu, and Ketu) move through twelve zodiac signs (9 x 12 = 108).

As the body is infused with prana, which is a derivative of sunlight, the solar flow takes place. For solar flows I encourage taking into account where the Sun is in both sidereal and tropical transits, as well as the sign of the Sun in the natal chart (if it's a flow designed for a single person).

Many solar flows include elements from Surya Namaskar (Sun Salute), pictured here. It's traditional on the solstice days to practice 108 Surya Namaskars, since 108 is a sacred number in yoga. Some traditions encourage performing only nine, since there are 12 postures in a traditional Surya Namaskar and 12 x 9 = 108. A solar cycle involves the Sun moving through the 12 signs, so the inclusion of 12 postures is representative of each of the energetic signatures of the Sun throughout any solar cycle. Surya Namaskar's numerology, along with its linear, heating, and uplifting qualities, makes it a cornerstone of any physical solar-encoded yoga practice. If you're ever in doubt when planning a solar flow, include Surya Namaskar.

Surya Namaskar (Sun Salute)

Many lunar flows include elements from Chandra Namaskar, pictured here. It's advisable to practice Chandra Namaskar on days surrounding the full and new Moon. Like Surya Namaskar, Chandra Namaskar also connects to the number twelve in relationship to the zodiac.

Chandra Namaskar is focused on the lower body and moves in a circular motion that mirrors or reverses the initial postures in the sequence. This differs from Surya Namaskar, which is uplifting and moves in a linear fashion, always facing the same direction.

Chandra Namaskar's circular, reflective qualities make it a cornerstone of any physical lunar-encoded yoga practice. If you're ever in doubt when planning a lunar flow, include Chandra Namaskar.

Lunar flows tend to be connected to the Moon Salute, and often incorporate elements from yin or restorative yoga. To practice lunar yoga means to ground energy into the body and allow the physical form of the body to flow, moving emotion and energy through your form. As release and integration take place, lunar energy is integrated to be life-supporting. For lunar flows I encourage taking into account the phase of the Moon, where the Moon is in both sidereal and tropical transits, and the phase and sign of the Moon in the natal chart (if it's a flow designed for a single person).

Chandra Namaskar (Moon Salute)

Planetary Practices

Planetary practices operate in honor of a particular planet, in order to more fully invite that planet's energetic signature into the body and life experience. Certain practices are more appropriate for particular planets. When planning planetary flows, take into account the transiting planet's location, as well as the planet's location in the natal chart (if it's a flow designed for a single person). Due to the difference in nature of the inner and outer planets, only inner planetary practices will be discussed, as these planets are the ones which predominate the connection with the body.

☿ Mercury

To integrate Mercury into your practice, take into account where transiting Mercury is in the zodiac and include postures that stabilize and generate health in the physical correspondences to Mercury's transit. You may remember that Mercury's glyph depicts the nadis, which can be enlivened and purified through pranayama. As well, Mercury rules Gemini, the sign related to the lungs and nervous system. From these references, we see that Mercury is specifically related to the flow of breath, so incorporating breathwork is one of the most important practices when connecting with Mercury through yoga. Practicing yoga to integrate Mercury will help you clarify your thoughts, speech, and communication, as well as give you clarity and free-flowing breath. It can also help you focus your attention.

♀ Venus

To integrate Venus into your practice, take into account where transiting Venus is in the zodiac and include postures that stabilize and generate health in the physical correspondences to her transit. Venus is specifically connected to the heart chakra, so incorporating heart opening is an important practice when connecting with Venus through yoga. Be sure to open the front and back of the heart space. Practicing yoga to integrate Venus will help you create harmony in your relationship with yourself and others, as well as increase abundance and beauty.

♂ Mars

To integrate Mars into your practice, take into account where transiting Mars is in the zodiac and include postures that stabilize and generate health in the physical correspondences to his transit. Mars is specifically connected to physical vitality and the will, so incorporating asana is an important practice when connecting with Mars through yoga. Practicing yoga to integrate Mars will help you increase physical vitality, heal anger, and hone your will.

♃ Jupiter

To integrate Jupiter into your practice, take into account where transiting Jupiter is in the zodiac and include postures that stabilize and generate health in the physical correspondences to his transit. Jupiter is specifically connected to learning and expanding your consciousness, so incorporating philosophy, study, or ritual is ideal when connecting with Jupiter through yoga. Practicing yoga to integrate Jupiter will help you increase knowledge, positivity, and your ability to discern what is beneficial in life.

♄ Saturn

To integrate Saturn into your practice, take into account where transiting Saturn is in the zodiac and include postures that stabilize and generate health in the physical correspondences to his transit. Saturn is specifically connected to structure and boundary lines such as breath retention, fasting, and bandhas. So if they are in your practice, incorporate breath retention, bandhas, awareness of skeletal placement, and austerities to connect your practice to Saturn. Practicing yoga to integrate Saturn will help you experience the higher potencies of life while in your embodied state and will build your capacity to both direct and see through the physical aspects of life.

Kosha Practices and Elemental Practices

Kosha practices and elemental practices create harmony with the earth, water, fire, air, and ether within you. Generally, when practicing kosha flows, begin with the earth element, and move steadily into more and more subtle practices until you enter into the element of etheric practice. Begin with earth through steady, grounding postures that allow you to move slowly and create a steady awareness of your form in space. Follow this with water, incorporating fluid asanas and flowing sequences of postures. Continue into fire, adding in heating elements and fiery holds in postures that activate muscle. Finally, move into air, finding ways to practice pranayama and meditation, stilling the mind. Eventually move into ether through deep meditation followed by savasana.

Chart Practices

To create a practice for a chart, first take into account whether you're flowing for the entire chart or with the intent to balance a particular area. For example, some individuals have a discrete goal in mind such as harnessing their creativity, gaining clarity in their career, or creating harmony in their relationships. All of these will call for practices specific to placements relating to these themes.

If you are flowing for a theme, examine all placements and aspects connected with that theme and create a practice to stabilize and energize those placements in an integrated way. If you are flowing more generally for a chart, examine the key personal planets and aspect patterns that create the energetic make-up of the chart. Themes and related practices will occur to you as you study the chart.

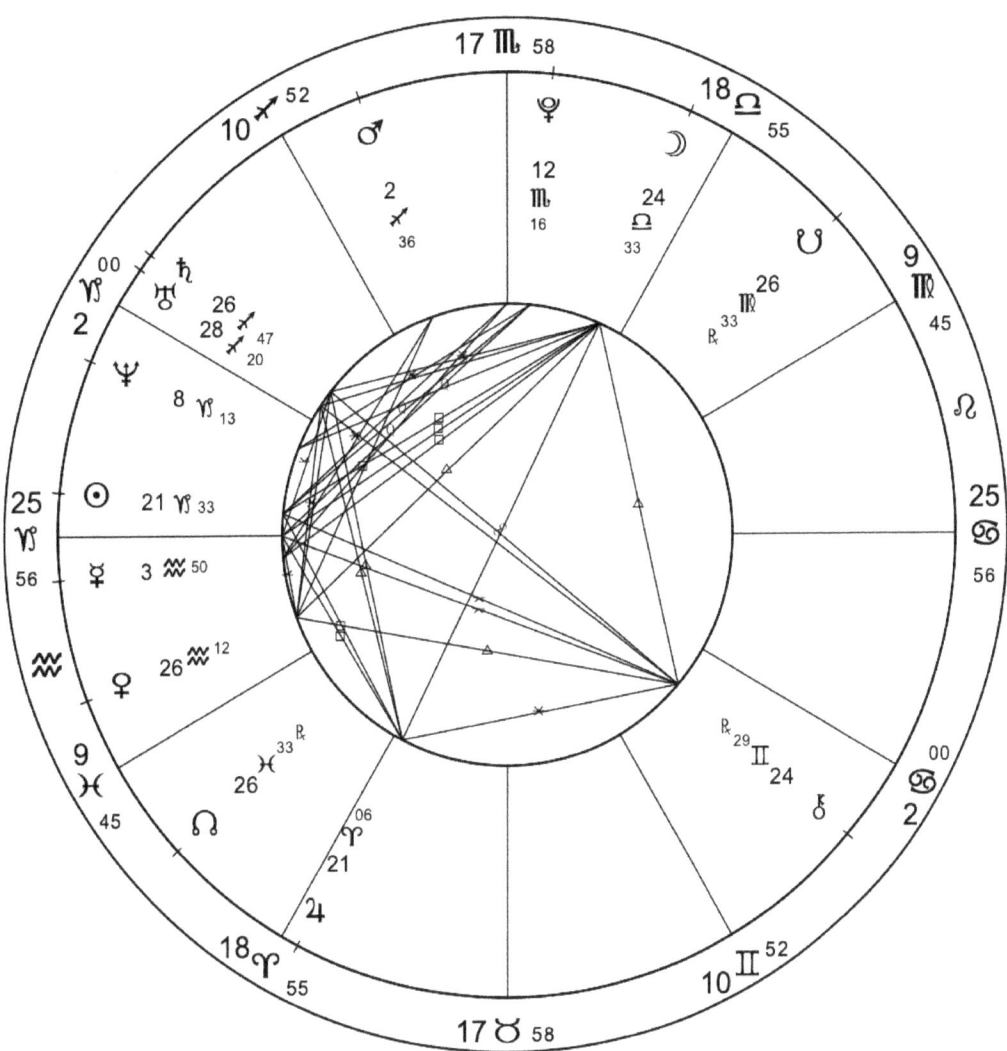

Example: Lauren

Here is a sample chart from a woman named Lauren. Lauren is in her mid-30s and has an existing physical yoga practice, as well as an interest in yoga philosophy and meditation. Let's imagine she wants help with a particular issue. Perhaps she is going through a period of time in which her inner light seems to be dampened. She has not been feeling like herself, and at times she feels a sense of hopelessness as she tries to both be herself and fit into the world. She comes to AstroYoga looking for help restoring the sense of aliveness and vitality she felt at other moments in her life.

A quick glance at this chart reveals the crux of this issue, as well as a set of practices to restore her vitality. Generally, a lack of zest in life has to do with the Sun, Jupiter, or Venus. Because she mentioned not feeling like herself, it's likely the Sun is involved, or possibly the chart ruler, which in this case is Saturn. Upon examining her chart, we see there is a T-Square to the Sun in Capricorn involving Jupiter in Aries and the Moon in Libra. Here we see a tendency for energy to get stuck, and a need to create a practice that will help energy flow more freely among these planets. The T Square takes place between the third, ninth, and twelfth houses, and here we see the themes of losing the sense of expansion she felt in childhood (3rd house Jupiter), while experiencing a sense of despondency in articulating herself in the world (9th house Moon), and needing to reclaim her personal power against an ever-changing world (12th house Sun). Because the Sun also conjoins the ascendant, this will have to do with both her personal identity and her spiritual self, which is perhaps why she turned to AstroYoga in the first place.

As well, we see that toward the end of the eleventh house, her chart ruler Saturn is conjoining Uranus in Sagittarius. This conjunction is one that also warrants our attention in this example, as Saturn likes to form and restrict, while Uranus likes to break apart and free. All of these placements should be considered when addressing her query.

To create a flow for these placements, consider that she is going to need a structured, yet adaptable, practice in order to suit her Uranus/Saturn conjunction. As well, she should be given information on the philosophy behind why she's doing what she's doing, as her prominent Jupiter and Sagittarius placements are likely to rebel without some degree of understanding. As such, I'd suggest creating a modular practice that can be adapted to suit her day. For example, I would create a ten minute asana flow that can be mixed and matched with breath, meditation, or a contemplation on yoga philosophy.

For the physical practice, it's essential to include an awareness of structure for the Saturn and Capricorn placements, as well as a sense of balance and beauty for the lunar Libra placement.

Here is the practice I would offer Lauren:

Start with standing postures that emphasize structural alignment with the bones and open and support the hips, while creating strength in the low back. Keep the head in awareness and alignment and focus the gaze in these postures. This will combine the Sagittarius, Capricorn, Aries, and Libra placements in this formation. Suggested postures: Three rounds of Surya Namaskar A (Sun Salute A). Follow this with virabhadrasana II (warrior II), trikonasana (triangle pose), parsvakonasana (side angle pose). Hold each posture for 3-7 breaths.

Next, add in some fluidity to support the lunar principle and to break up any rigidity from Saturn or Capricorn. You want these placements to emphasize structure, not create rigidity in the form. Here I would suggest a uttanasana (forward fold) with bent knees, swaying the body and taking deep breaths.

At this point, the body is prepared for the next segment of practice. Here I would suggest breathwork. Because Lauren is looking to build vitality and alleviate despondency, the emphasis should be on solar, heating breaths, followed by balancing breaths. Here I would suggest bhastrika pranayama (bellows breath), kapalabhati (skull shining breath), and nadi shodhana (alternate nostril breath). After these three, it's advisable to take several deep breaths in and out the nose.

After that, I'd offer possibilities. If she has time, she could add in some yoga philosophy, chanting, or meditation. The practice ends with savasana.

When planning practices for particular chart activation, it's good to check in after a week or two of practice to make any necessary adjustments. Keep in mind that if you are clearing stagnant energy, there could be a period of time in which you feel worse, not better, as old samskaras (latent impressions in the body) clear away. Clearing samskaras generally feels emotional, not physical, and there should be no pain in the physical body. Make adjustments to intensify, balance, or lessen the practice's impact, as necessary.

Transit Flows

Flowing for a transit chart is similar to flowing for a personal chart, except with the transit chart you practice with an understanding of how long particular transits will last. Additionally, if you're planning a flow for a particular person, you may take into account their natal chart as it relates to the transits.

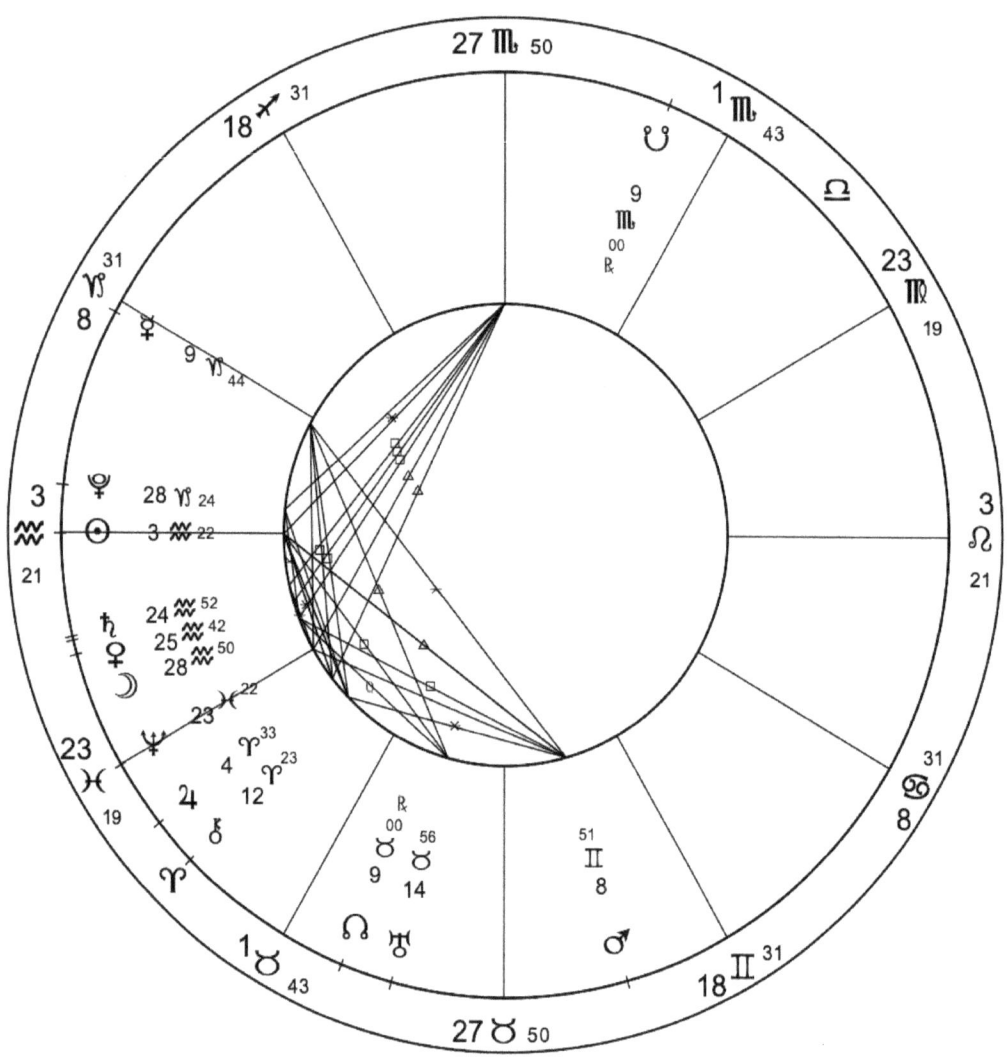

Example: This Book's Launch Date

To practice for transits, you could pick any date and examine the particular transits emphasized at that moment. For the purposes of this book, I'm examining the launch date for this book, and imagining that we are designing an asana class for the general public, without consideration of how it is affecting individual charts. This will be the case for most class practices you design.

In this chart, we see a concentrated theme in Aquarius, containing four primary planets: the Sun, Saturn, Venus, and the Moon. As well, it's notable that the north node and Uranus are in a loose conjunction in Taurus, and Chiron is in Aries. With this chart, I'd emphasize the stellium in Aquarius, while placing the head and neck in good alignment, so as to promote wellbeing in Taurus and Aries.

Since Aquarius rules the circulation and the ankles, asanas should be chosen that promote health in these areas. And, since planets here are connected with the root, heart, and third eye chakras, a theme emerges. This theme traces the connection among material embodiment in the root, the spark of ultimate love in the heart, and the light of conscious awareness in the third eye space.

Therefore, I would include asanas that tie these chakras together. An obvious choice would be the natarajasana (king dancer pose). This opens the heart and strengthens the ankles, all while embodying the personification of the awakened third eye space. A sequence of postures leading up to this pose would be ideal for the average asana class. Postures that would easily align could include rooted postures that open the hips such as virabhadrasana II (warrior II), heart-centered postures that prepare the spine and chest for deeper heart opening such as bhujangasana (cobra pose) or salambasana (locust pose), and postures that support healthy ankles and circulation such as vrksasana (tree pose) or vyaghrasana (tiger pose). These are simply for illustrative purposes, you could certainly come up with more postures along these lines.

From the above considerations, a class or personal sequence easily emerges, and you'll have something to teach or practice that is likely to help align the energies of each practitioner with the timing of that particular moment.

Beyond Asana

As you continue in AstroYoga, subtler techniques will become more effective means for practicing in a way that actively engages the forces spoken about in this book. For mudra and mantra practices, as well as a deep study of the chakras, it's important to find an authentic teacher in an initiatory tradition with true knowledge of these paths. Such teachers are able to teach you your individual practice in a way that will be effective for you.

The dictum that when the student is ready the teacher appears isn't just a saying. This also means that when the teacher appears to you, you will be ready to embark on deeper paths of study and practice. Always be cautious and make sure the teachers you work with are grounded in truth. You can generally tell false teachers by their grandiose promises that the path will be easy and quick.

In the coming age, many people will find or be found by their teachers, and steady, authentic practice will become increasingly more common. All of humanity will ultimately succeed in walking this path together.

About the Author

Emily Ridout is an AstroYoga Specialist and Astrologer. She's spent the last 13 years honing her AstroYoga technique and counseling clients. She's been featured in *Women's Health*, *Reader's Digest*, *Yoga Journal*, and *Well + Good*, and she holds a B.A. (Indiana University) and M.A. (University of Oregon) in Folklore, as well as three yoga certifications from India and the United States. You can find her at emilyridout.com or out hiking in the mountains with her dog Wally.

www.ingramcontent.com/pod-product-compliance
Lightning Source LLC
Chambersburg PA
CBHW042014120526
44592CB00043B/2858